SOUND

TASK CARD SERIES

Conceived and written by
RON MARSON

Illustrated by
PEG MARSON

342 S Plumas Street
Willows, CA 95988

www.topscience.org

WHAT CAN YOU COPY?

Dear Educator,

Please honor our copyright restrictions. We offer liberal options and guidelines below with the intention of balancing your needs with ours. When you buy these labs and use them for your own teaching, you sustain our work. If you "loan" or circulate copies to others without compensating TOPS, you squeeze us financially, and make it harder for our small non-profit to survive. Our well-being rests in your hands. Please help us keep our low-cost, creative lessons available to students everywhere. Thank you!

PURCHASE, ROYALTY and LICENSE OPTIONS

TEACHERS, HOMESCHOOLERS, LIBRARIES:

We do all we can to keep our prices low. Like any business, we have ongoing expenses to meet. We trust our users to observe the terms of our copyright restrictions. While we prefer that all users purchase their own TOPS labs, we accept that real-life situations sometimes call for flexibility.

Reselling, trading, or loaning our materials is prohibited unless one or both parties contribute an Honor System Royalty as fair compensation for value received. We suggest the following amounts – let your conscience be your guide.

HONOR SYSTEM ROYALTIES: If making copies from a library, or sharing copies with colleagues, please calculate their value at 50 cents per lesson, or 25 cents for homeschoolers. This contribution may be made at our website or by mail (addresses at the bottom of this page). Any additional tax-deductible contributions to make our ongoing work possible will be accepted gratefully and used well.

Please follow through promptly on your good intentions. Stay legal, and do the right thing.

SCHOOLS, DISTRICTS, and HOMESCHOOL CO-OPS:

PURCHASE Option: Order a book in quantities equal to the number of target classrooms or homes, and receive quantity discounts. If you order 5 books or downloads, for example, then you have unrestricted use of this curriculum for any 5 classrooms or families per year for the life of your institution or co-op.

2-9 copies of any title: 90% of current catalog price + shipping.
10+ copies of any title: 80% of current catalog price + shipping.

ROYALTY/LICENSE Option: Purchase just one book or download *plus* photocopy or printing rights for a designated number of classrooms or families. If you pay for 5 additional Licenses, for example, then you have purchased reproduction rights for an entire book or download edition for any **6** classrooms or families per year for the life of your institution or co-op.

1-9 Licenses: 70% of current catalog price per designated classroom or home.
10+ Licenses: 60% of current catalog price per designated classroom or home.

WORKSHOPS and TEACHER TRAINING PROGRAMS:

We are grateful to all of you who spread the word about TOPS. Please limit copies to only those lessons you will be using, and collect all copyrighted materials afterward. No take-home copies, please. Copies of copies are strictly prohibited.

Copyright © 1990 by TOPS Learning Systems. All rights reserved. This material is created/printed/transmitted in the United States of America. No part of this program may be used, reproduced, or transmitted in any manner whatsoever without written permission from the publisher, *except as explicitly stated above and below*:

The *original owner* of this book or digital download is permitted to make multiple copies of all **student materials** for personal teaching use, provided all reproductions bear copyright notice. A purchasing school or homeschool co-op may assign **one** purchased book or digital download to **one** teacher, classroom, family, or study group **per year**. Reproduction of student materials from libraries is permitted if the user compensates TOPS as outlined above. Reproduction of any copyrighted materials for commercial sale is prohibited.

For licensing, honor system royalty payments, contact: **www.TOPScience.org**; or **TOPS Learning Systems 342 S Plumas St, Willows CA 95988**; or inquire at **customerservice@topscience.org**

ISBN 978-0-941008-88-4

CONTENTS

 ## PART I — INTRODUCTION

- A. A TOPS Model for Effective Science Teaching
- C. Getting Ready
- D. Gathering Materials
- E. Sequencing Task Cards
- F. Long Range Objectives
- G. Review / Test Questions

 ## PART II — TEACHING NOTES

CORE CURRICULUM
1. Sources of Sound
2. Pencil Waves
3. Hair Pin Waves
4. Frequency
5. Wave Train
6. Tuning Fork Waves
7. Intensity
8. Pitch
9. Sound Mediums
10. Two Kinds of Waves
11. Longitudinal Waves
12. Pitch Problem (1)
13. Pitch Problem (2)

ENRICHMENT CURRICULUM
14. Resonance
15. Beats
16. Octave Rules
17. How Low Can You Go?
18. On the Record
19. Reed Music
20. Speed of Sound

 ## PART III — REPRODUCIBLE STUDENT TASK CARDS

Task Cards 1-20
Supplementary Page — Frequency Strips, Metric Rulers

A TOPS Model for Effective Science Teaching...

If science were only a set of explanations and a collection of facts, you could teach it with blackboard and chalk. You could assign students to read chapters and answer the questions that followed. Good students would take notes, read the text, turn in assignments, then give you all this information back again on a final exam. Science is traditionally taught in this manner. Everybody learns the same body of information at the same time. Class togetherness is preserved.

But science is more than this.

Science is also process — a dynamic interaction of rational inquiry and creative play. Scientists probe, poke, handle, observe, question, think up theories, test ideas, jump to conclusions, make mistakes, revise, synthesize, communicate, disagree and discover. Students can understand science as process only if they are free to think and act like scientists, in a classroom that recognizes and honors individual differences.

Science is *both* a traditional body of knowledge *and* an individualized process of creative inquiry. Science as process cannot ignore tradition. We stand on the shoulders of those who have gone before. If each generation reinvents the wheel, there is no time to discover the stars. Nor can traditional science continue to evolve and redefine itself without process. Science without this cutting edge of discovery is a static, dead thing.

Here is a teaching model that combines the best of both elements into one integrated whole. It is only a model. Like any scientific theory, it must give way over time to new and better ideas. We challenge you to incorporate this TOPS model into your own teaching practice. Change it and make it better so it works for you.

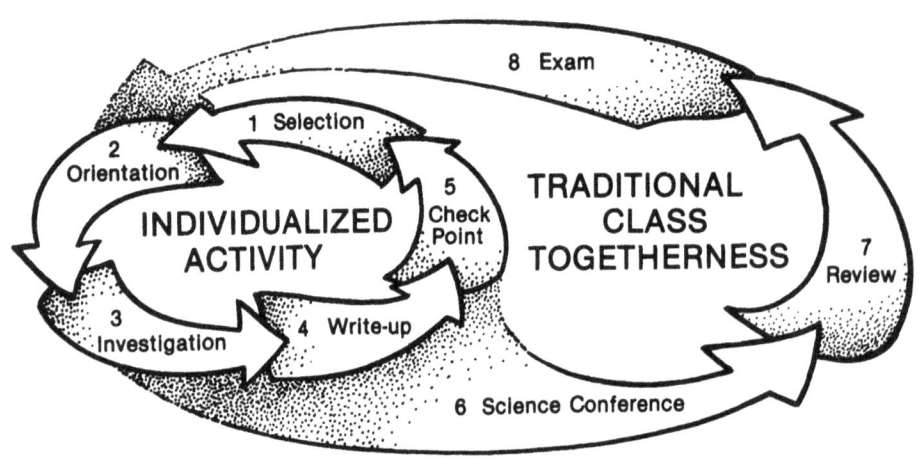

1. SELECTION

Doing TOPS is as easy as selecting the first task card and doing what it says, then the second, then the third, and so on. Working at their own pace, students fall into a natural routine that creates stability and order. They still have questions and problems, to be sure, but students know where they are and where they need to go.

Students generally select task cards in sequence because new concepts build on old ones in a specific order. There are, however, exceptions to this rule: students might *skip* a task that is not challenging; *repeat* a task with doubtful results; *add* a task of their own design to answer original "what would happen if" questions.

2. ORIENTATION

Many students will simply read a task card and immediately understand what to do. Others will require further verbal interpretation. Identify poor readers in your class. When they ask, "What does this mean?" they may be asking in reality, "Will you please read this card aloud?"

With such a diverse range of talent among students, how can you individualize activity and still hope to finish this module as a cohesive group? It's easy. By the time your most advanced students have completed all the task cards, including the enrichment series at the end, your slower students have at least completed the basic core curriculum. This core provides the common background so necessary for meaningful discussion, review and testing on a class basis.

3. INVESTIGATION

Students work through the task cards independently and cooperatively. They follow their own experimental strategies and help each other. You encourage this behavior by helping students only *after* they have tried to help themselves. As a resource person, you work to stay *out* of the center of attention, answering student questions rather than posing teacher questions.

When you need to speak to everyone at once, it is appropriate to interrupt individual task card activity and address the whole class, rather than repeat yourself over and over again. If you plan ahead, you'll find that most interruptions can fit into brief introductory remarks at the beginning of each new period.

4. WRITE-UP

Task cards ask students to explain the "how and why" of things. Write-ups are brief and to the point. Students may accelerate their pace through the task cards by writing these reports out of class.

Students may work alone or in cooperative lab groups. But each one must prepare an original write-up. These must be brought to the teacher for approval as soon as they are completed. Avoid dealing with too many write-ups near the end of the module, by enforcing this simple rule: each write-up must be approved *before* continuing on to the next task card.

5. CHECK POINT

The student and teacher evaluate each write-up together on a pass/no-pass basis. (Thus no time is wasted haggling over grades.) If the student has made reasonable effort consistent with individual ability, the write-up is checked off on a progress chart and included in the student's personal assignment folder or notebook kept on file in class.

Because the student is present when you evaluate, feedback is immediate and effective. A few seconds of this direct student-teacher interaction is surely more effective than 5 minutes worth of margin notes that students may or may not heed. Remember, you don't have to point out every error. Zero in on particulars. If reasonable effort has not been made, direct students to make specific improvements, and see you again for a follow-up check point.

A responsible lab assistant can double the amount of individual attention each student receives. If he or she is mature and respected by your students, have the assistant check the even-numbered write-ups while you check the odd ones. This will balance the work load and insure that all students receive equal treatment.

6. SCIENCE CONFERENCE

After individualized task card activity has ended, this is a time for students to come together, to discuss experimental results, to debate and draw conclusions. Slower students learn about the enrichment activities of faster students. Those who did original investigations, or made unusual discoveries, share this information with their peers, just like scientists at a real conference. This conference is open to films, newspaper articles and community speakers. It is a perfect time to consider the technological and social implications of the topic you are studying.

7. READ AND REVIEW

Does your school have an adopted science textbook? Do parts of your science syllabus still need to be covered? Now is the time to integrate other traditional science resources into your overall program. Your students already share a common background of hands-on lab work. With this shared base of experience, they can now read the text with greater understanding, think and problem-solve more successfully, communicate more effectively.

You might spend just a day on this step or an entire week. Finish with a review of key concepts in preparation for the final exam. Test questions in this module provide an excellent basis for discussion and study.

8. EXAM

Use any combination of the review/test questions, plus questions of your own, to determine how well students have mastered the concepts they've been learning. Those who finish your exam early might begin work on the first activity in the next new TOPS module.

Now that your class has completed a major TOPS learning cycle, it's time to start fresh with a brand new topic. Those who messed up and got behind don't need to stay there. Everyone begins the new topic on an equal footing. This frequent change of pace encourages your students to work hard, to enjoy what they learn, and thereby grow in scientific literacy.

GETTING READY

Here is a checklist of things to think about and preparations to make before your first lesson.

☐ Decide if this TOPS module is the best one to teach next.

TOPS modules are flexible. They can generally be scheduled in any order to meet your own class needs. Some lessons within certain modules, however, do require basic math skills or a knowledge of fundamental laboratory techniques. Review the task cards in this module now if you are not yet familiar with them. Decide whether you should teach any of these other TOPS modules first: *Measuring Length, Graphing, Metric Measure, Weighing* or *Electricity* (before *Magnetism*). It may be that your students already possess these requisite skills or that you can compensate with extra class discussion or special assistance.

☐ Number your task card masters in pencil.

The small number printed in the lower right corner of each task card shows its position within the overall series. If this ordering fits your schedule, copy each number into the blank parentheses directly above it at the top of the card. Be sure to use pencil rather than ink. You may decide to revise, upgrade or rearrange these task cards next time you teach this module. To do this, write your own better ideas on blank 4 x 6 index cards, and renumber them into the task card sequence wherever they fit best. In this manner, your curriculum will adapt and grow as you do.

☐ Copy your task card masters.

You have our permission to reproduce these task cards, for as long as you teach, with only 1 restriction: please limit the distribution of copies you make to the students you personally teach. Encourage other teachers who want to use this module to purchase their *own* copy. This supports TOPS financially, enabling us to continue publishing new TOPS modules for you. For a full list of task card options, please turn to the first task card masters numbered "cards 1-2."

☐ Collect needed materials.

Please see the opposite page.

☐ Organize a way to track completed assignment.

Keep write-ups on file in class. If you lack a vertical file, a box with a brick will serve. File folders or notebooks both make suitable assignment organizers. Students will feel a sense of accomplishment as they see their file folders grow heavy, or their notebooks fill up, with completed assignments. Easy reference and convenient review are assured, since all papers remain in one place.

Ask students to staple a sheet of numbered graph paper to the inside front cover of their file folder or notebook. Use this paper to track each student's progress through the module. Simply initial the corresponding task card number as students turn in each assignment.

☐ Review safety procedures.

Most TOPS experiments are safe even for small children. Certain lessons, however, require heat from a candle flame or Bunsen burner. Others require students to handle sharp objects like scissors, straight pins and razor blades. These task cards should not be attempted by immature students unless they are closely supervised. You might choose instead to turn these experiments into teacher demonstrations.

Unusual hazards are noted in the teaching notes and task cards where appropriate. But the curriculum cannot anticipate irresponsible behavior or negligence. It is ultimately the teacher's responsibility to see that common sense safety rules are followed at all times. Begin with these basic safety rules:
  1. Eye Protection: Wear safety goggles when heating liquids or solids to high temperatures.
  2. Poisons: Never taste anything unless told to do so.
  3. Fire: Keep loose hair or clothing away from flames. Point test tubes which are heating away from your face and your neighbor's.
  4. Glass Tubing: Don't force through stoppers. (The teacher should fit glass tubes to stoppers in advance, using a lubricant.)
  5. Gas: Light the match first, before turning on the gas.

☐ Communicate your grading expectations.

Whatever your philosophy of grading, your students need to understand the standards you expect and how they will be assessed. Here is a grading scheme that counts individual effort, attitude and overall achievement. We think these 3 components deserve equal weight:
  1. Pace (effort): Tally the number of check points you have initialed on the graph paper attached to each student's file folder or science notebook. Low ability students should be able to keep pace with gifted students, since write-ups are evaluated relative to individual performance standards. Students with absences or those who tend to work at a slow pace may (or may not) choose to overcome this disadvantage by assigning themselves more homework out of class.
  2. Participation (attitude): This is a subjective grade assigned to reflect each student's attitude and class behavior. Active participators who work to capacity receive high marks. Inactive onlookers, who waste time in class and copy the results of others, receive low marks.
  3. Exam (achievement): Task cards point toward generalizations that provide a base for hypothesizing and predicting. A final test over the entire module determines whether students understand relevant theory and can apply it in a predictive way.

Gathering Materials

Listed below is everything you'll need to teach this module. You already have many of these items. The rest are available from your supermarket, drugstore and hardware store. Laboratory supplies may be ordered through a science supply catalog. Hobby stores also carry basic science equipment.

Keep this classification key in mind as you review what's needed:

special in-a-box materials:	general on-the-shelf materials:
Italic type suggests that these materials are unusual. Keep these specialty items in a separate box. After you finish teaching this module, label the box for storage and put it away, ready to use again the next time you teach this module.	Normal type suggests that these materials are common. Keep these basics on shelves or in drawers that are readily accessible to your students. The next TOPS module you teach will likely utilize many of these same materials.
(substituted materials):	*optional materials:
A parentheses following any item suggests a ready substitute. These alternatives may work just as well as the original, perhaps better. Don't be afraid to improvise, to make do with what you have.	An asterisk sets these items apart. They are nice to have, but you can easily live without them. They are probably not worth an extra trip, unless you are gathering other materials as well.

Everything is listed in order of first use. Start gathering at the top of this list and work down. Ask students to bring recycled items from home. The teaching notes may occasionally suggest additional student activity under the heading "Extensions." Materials for these optional experiments are listed neither here nor in the teaching notes. Read the extension itself to find out what new materials, if any, are required.

Needed quantities depend on how many students you have, how you organize them into activity groups, and how you teach. Decide which of these 3 estimates best applies to you, then adjust quantities up or down as necessary:

$Q_1 / Q_2 / Q_3$
- **Single Student:** Enough for 1 student to do all the experiments.
- **Individualized Approach:** Enough for 30 students informally working in 10 lab groups, all self-paced.
- **Traditional Approach:** Enough for 30 students, organized into 10 lab groups, all doing the same lesson.

KEY:	*special in-a-box materials* (substituted materials)	general on-the-shelf materials *optional materials

$Q_1 / Q_2 / Q_3$

1 / 15 / 30	*tuning forks* — long (low) ones have the widest application in this module; at least some should be stamped to identify their vibrating frequency		1 / 10 / 10	meter sticks or other metric rulers
			1 / 1 / 1	a wall clock with second-hand sweep (student wrist watches)
1 / 10 / 10	drinking glasses or beakers		1 / 10 / 10	*hand calculators
4 / 20 / 40	*bobby pins*		1 / 3 / 10	Ping-Pong balls (marbles)
4 / 40 / 40	medium sized cans		1 / 6 / 10	dinner forks (spoons)
2 / 10 / 20	soda bottles or equivalent		1 / 1 / 1	roll of string
1 / 10 / 10	scissors		1 / 5 / 10	*hammer and nails — needed for punching holes in cans; these can be omitted if this operation is completed in advance
4 / 40 / 40	4x6 index cards			
1 / 2 / 2	rolls adding-machine tape		7 / 70 / 70	straight plastic straws
2 / 20 / 20	straight pins		.2 / 1 / 2	cups of clay
1 / 2 / 2	rolls masking tape		2 / 15 / 20	paper clips
3 / 15 / 30	clothespins		1 / 1 / 1	bottles cooking oil (baby oil)
3 / 30 / 30	rubber bands		1 / 1 / 1	roll of thin bare wire — iron, copper or aluminum; 22 gauge is appropriate
1 / 1 / 1	*jar petroleum jelly*			
1 / 10 / 10	panes of glass approximately 10x10 cm; microscope slides will serve in a pinch; hand mirrors work nearly as well		1 / 1 / 1	*wire cutters
			1 / 4 / 10	tuna fish cans or equivalent
			1 / 4 / 10	*old records*
1 / 20 / 50	pennies		1 / 1 / 1	paper punch
1 / 1 / 1	spool of thread		1 / 1 / 1	*pairs of wood blocks (a spoon and pan)*

D

Sequencing Task Cards

This logic tree shows how all the task cards in this module tie together. In general, students begin at the trunk of the tree and work up through the related branches. As the diagram suggests, the way to upper level activities leads up from lower level activities.

At the teacher's discretion, certain activities can be omitted or sequences changed to meet specific class needs. The only activities that must be completed in sequence are indicated by leaves that open *vertically* into the ones above them. In these cases the lower activity is a prerequisite to the upper.

When possible, students should complete the task cards in the same sequence as numbered. If time is short, however, or certain students need to catch up, you can use the logic tree to identify concept-related *horizontal* activities. Some of these might be omitted since they serve only to reinforce learned concepts rather than introduce new ones.

On the other hand, if students complete all the activities at a certain horizontal concept level, then experience difficulty at the next higher level, you might go back down the logic tree to have students repeat specific key activities for greater reinforcement.

For whatever reason, when you wish to make sequence changes, you'll find this logic tree a valuable reference. Parentheses in the upper right corner of each task card allow you total flexibility. They are left blank so you can pencil in sequence numbers of your own choosing.

SOUND 18

Long-Range Objectives

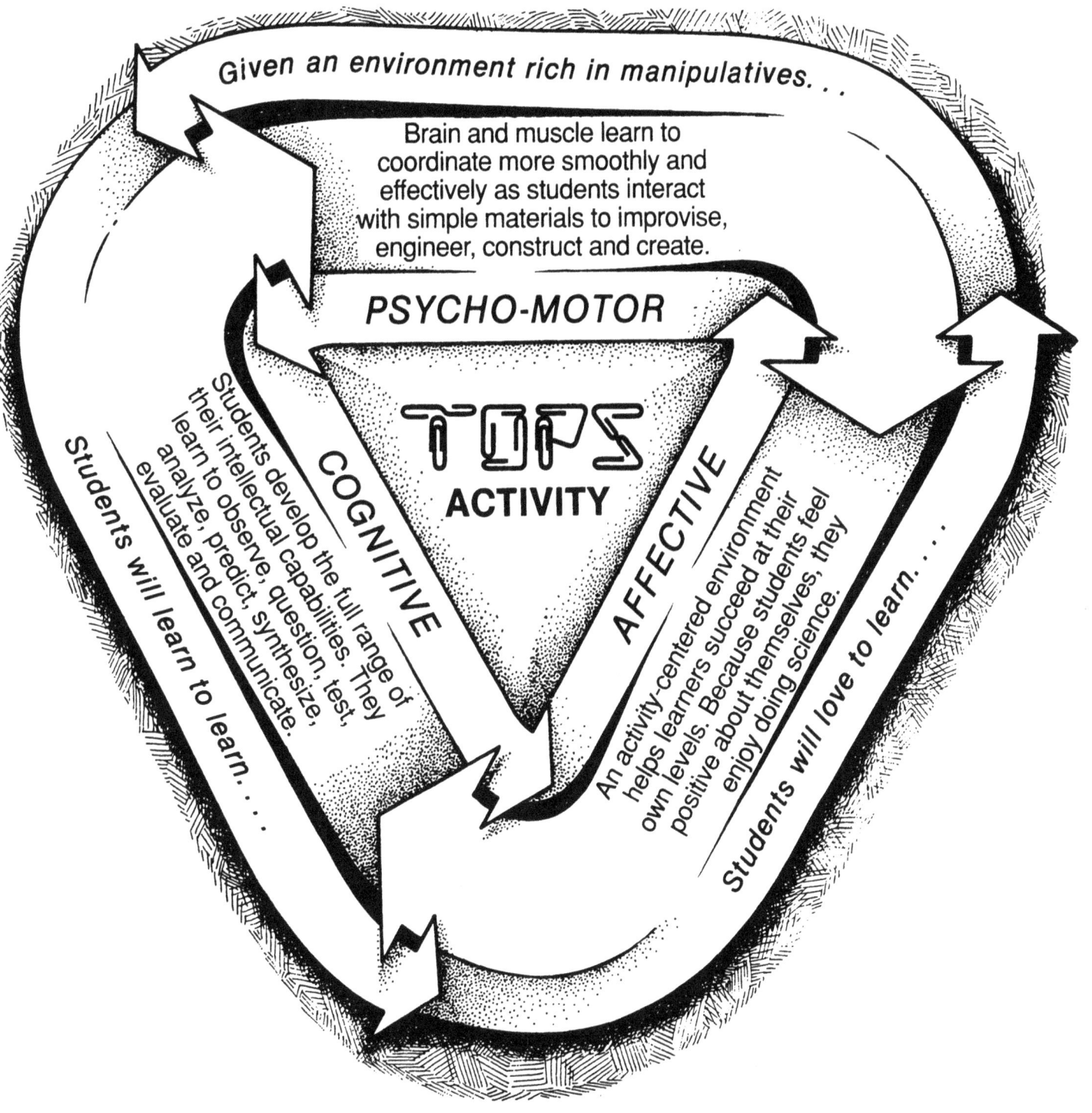

Review / Test Questions

Photocopy the questions below. On a separate sheet of blank paper, cut and paste those boxes you want to use as test questions. Include questions of your own design, as well. Crowd all these questions onto a single page for students to answer on another paper, or leave space for student responses after each question, as you wish. Duplicate a class set and your custom-made test is ready to use. Use leftover questions as a review in preparation for the final exam.

task 1
Flying insects buzz and hum. How do they produce these sounds?

task 2
A funnel of sand swings back and forth while sand pours out in a small steady stream from the bottom.

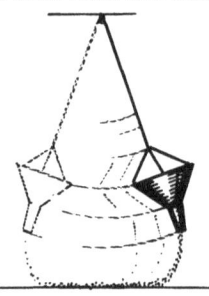

a. Explain how you would use this special pendulum to make sand waves on paper.
b. How would you alter the wavelength of your sand waves?

task 3
Each square on the grid measures 1 cm by 1 cm. What is the wavelength and amplitude of wave x? wave y?

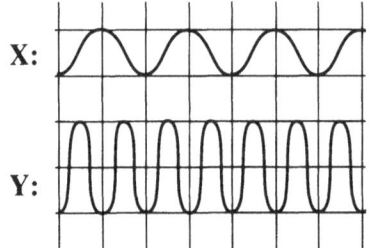

task 4
A tiny 1 cm pendulum vibrates about 300 cycles per minute. Find its frequency in Hertz units.

task 5-6
This 440 Hz vibration is recorded over a distance of 20 cm. How fast did the wave travel in cm/sec? in meters/sec?

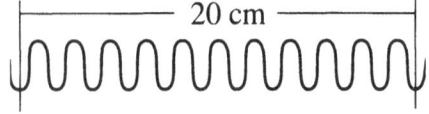

task 7-8
Which greased glass tracing was made with...
a. a low pitched tuning fork sounding at low intensity?
b. a high pitched tuning fork sounding at high intensity?
c. a high pitched tuning fork sounding at low intensity?

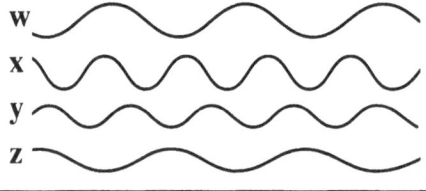

task 7-8
Why is the buzz of a bumble bee lower than the hum of a mosquito? Why is it louder?

task 8
Two tuning forks were moved together across greased glass, leaving these wave trains. If the higher fork vibrates at 256 Hz, what is the frequency of the lower fork?

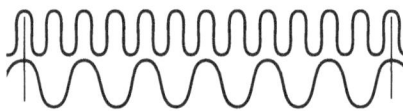

task 9
A meteor hits a space station orbiting high above Earth.
a. Do astronauts inside hear the sound of its impact? Explain.
b. Does an astronaut working nearby on the outside of the space station hear its impact?

task 10-11
How are ocean waves different from sound waves? Draw a representation of each.

task 12
Name 3 different ways to lower the pitch on a stringed instrument.

task 13
You are given some empty soda bottles. Describe how you can use these bottles to create ascending and descending notes.

task 14
Explain these observations using the idea of sympathetic pushes and resonance.
a. To push a car out of a ditch you should begin by rocking it to and fro.
b. When you sing in the shower, some notes sound louder than others.

task 15
A piano tuner hears 3 beats per second when comparing an A on the piano with standard A (in the same octave), on his tuning fork. If the tuning fork vibrates at 440 Hz, what is the frequency of the piano note? How should the tuner adjust the string to sound at the correct pitch?

task 16-17
Each wire is wedged tightly between 2 pieces of wood as shown. Background lines reveal their respective lengths. Which wires sound at the same note in different octaves? Explain how you know.

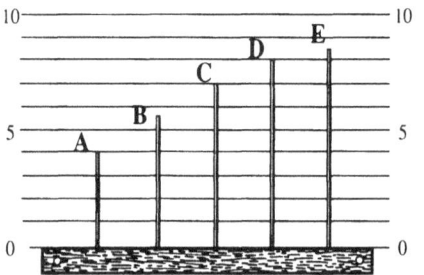

task 18
Spinning a record too fast raises the pitch of the music. Explain why.

task 19
Explain how a saxophone...
a. produces sound.
b. changes pitch.

task 20
A friend claps two boards together, with broad sweeping gestures, at a constant frequency of 2 Hz. Meanwhile you back away. After 80 meters, what you hear seems out of phase with what you see. After 160 meters, what you see and hear again seem to coincide.
a. Explain what is happening.
b. Calculate the speed of sound in this experiment.

Answers

task 1
Insects buzz and hum because their wings vibrate rapidly back and forth, producing sound.

task 2
a. While the pendulum is depositing sand to and fro in a straight line, pull a long sheet of paper underneath.
b. To make the sand waves shorter, pull the paper underneath more slowly, or shorten the pendulum so it swings at a higher frequency. To lengthen the sand waves, pull the paper underneath more rapidly, or lengthen the pendulum so it swings at a lower frequency.

task 3
Wave x has a length of 2 cm and an amplitude of 1/2 cm. Wave y has a length of 1 cm and an amplitude of 1 cm.

task 4
$$\frac{300 \text{ cycles}}{\text{min}} \times \frac{1 \text{ min}}{60 \text{ sec}} = 5 \text{ Hz}$$

task 5-6
A 20 cm interval contains 11 cycles:
$$\frac{440 \text{ cycles}}{\text{sec}} \times \frac{20 \text{ cm}}{11 \text{ cycles}} = 800 \text{ cm/sec} = 8 \text{ m/sec}$$

task 7-8
a. wave train z.
b. wave train x.
c. wave train y.

task 7-8
The bumble bee sounds lower because it beats its wings at a lower frequency than the mosquito. It sounds louder because it beats its wings with greater intensity, producing sound waves with higher amplitudes.

task 8
The lower fork vibrates 6 complete wavelengths while the higher fork vibrates 12.
$$\frac{6 \text{ waves}}{12 \text{ waves}} = \frac{\text{lower frequency}}{256 \text{ Hz}}$$
lower frequency = 128 Hz

task 9
a. Yes. The sound travels through the walls of the space station, then through the air inside where it can be heard by the inside astronauts.
b. Probably not. There is no air to carry the sound of the impact to the outside astronaut's ears. If she is physically connected to the ship in some way (by a lifeline, for example), the sound might conceivably pass through it into her suit.

task 10-11
Ocean waves are transverse. The water medium moves up and down, at right angles to the motion of the ocean waves.

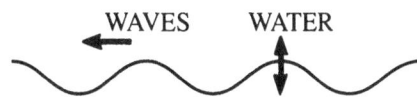

Sound waves are longitudinal. The air medium squeezes together (condenses) and expands (rarefies) in a back and forth motion that is parallel to the motion of the sound waves.

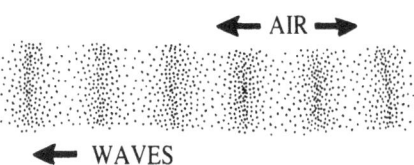

task 12
To lower the pitch...
a. decrease tension in the strings.
b. lengthen the strings.
c. use thicker strings.

task 13
Fill the bottles with increasing amounts of water.

(1) Blow across the top of each bottle, proceeding left to right. As the columns of air inside each bottle shorten, they vibrate at increasingly higher frequencies, sounding an ascending scale.
(2) Tap each bottle, again proceeding from left to right. The glass and water will vibrate at lower and lower frequencies as its total mass increases. This sounds a descending scale.

task 14
a. Resonating your pushes in sympathy with the car's own natural frequency continues to add more and more energy into the rocking car until it absorbs sufficient energy to rock free of the ditch.
b. Air in the shower vibrates at certain natural frequencies related to the dimensions of the enclosed space. When you sing certain notes having these same pitches, your voice is amplified by the surrounding air vibrating in sympathy, or resonating, at the same frequency.

task 15
The piano string vibrates at 437 Hz if it is flat, or 443 Hz if it is sharp. Both of these notes differ from the 440 Hz standard by 3 Hz.
The tuner should tighten or loosen the corresponding string very slightly until the beats slow and finally disappear.

task 16-17
Wires A and D sound on the same note 2 octaves apart, since the second is twice as long as the first. Wire B vibrates at the same note in the intermediate octave, since its length is a multiple of $\sqrt{2}$.
$$4 \times 2 = 8 = 5.7 \times \sqrt{2}$$

task 18
As the stylus moves over waves recorded between the record grooves, its vibrations duplicate that of the original sound. But if the record spins too rapidly, the needle vibrates at a higher frequency than normal, raising the pitch of the original sound.

task 19
a. A reed in the mouthpiece vibrates as you blow across it. This, in turn, resonates with the air inside the instrument to produce a tone.
b. Change the pitch by pressing the various finger pads. This opens holes in the instrument so that different volumes of air will vibrate at different frequencies, thus changing the pitch.

task 20
a. Sound travels slowly compared with nearly instantaneous light. At 80 meters, the sound of each clap doesn't reach your ears until you see your friend spreading his arms ready for the next clap. At 160 meters, each clap reaches your ears just as the next clap occurs, so that sight and sound are once again in phase.
b. $$\frac{160 \text{ meters}}{\text{clap}} \times \frac{2 \text{ claps}}{\text{sec}}$$
= 320 meters/second

TEACHING NOTES
For Activities 1-20

(TO) recognize that sound is produced by vibrating objects.

SOURCES OF SOUND Sound ( )

1. Do each experiment and write what you observe:

   a. Strike a tuning fork. While it is still humming, place the end in a glass of water.

   b. Straighten a bobby pin. Hold it against an inverted can while you strum the end.

   c. Touch your Adam's apple as you intermittently hum a low note.

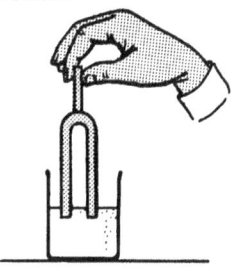 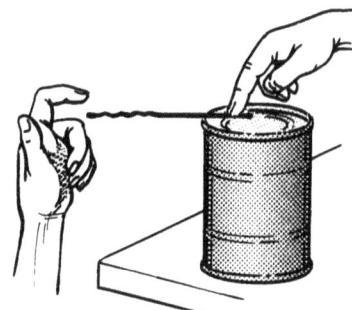 

2. What do tuning forks, hair pins, and vocal cords all do in order to produce sound?

3. Blow across the top of a soda bottle to make a note; tap on it with scissors. What vibrates to produce each sound?

© 1990 by TOPS Learning Systems

Answers / Notes

1a. The humming tuning fork splashes water. (*Keen observers may notice that standing waves are generated on the water's surface between the prongs of the vibrating fork.*)

1b. The end of the bobby pin rapidly vibrates back and forth in a blur of motion that produces a sound.

1c. The Adam's apple vibrates the finger tips each time a note is hummed.

2. All of these materials produce sound by vibrating rapidly back and forth.

3. Air inside the bottle vibrates when you blow across the top. The glass bottle itself vibrates when tapped by the scissors. (*If there is disagreement over the source of the sound, don't rush in to settle it with the "right" answer. Value uncertainty as an opportunity to think, reexamine the evidence and learn something new.*)

Materials

☐ A tuning fork.
☐ A glass or beaker filled with water.
☐ A "bobby" pin. These are not as common as they were 20 or 30 years ago, but are still sold in drug and variety stores.
☐ A can. Empty medium-sized cans, washed with labels removed, have wide application in this module.
☐ A soda bottle or equivalent small-necked bottle. Test tubes work too, if you can tolerate the loud, shrill whistle.
☐ Scissors.

(TO) build a device that generates waves. To produce waves of different lengths.

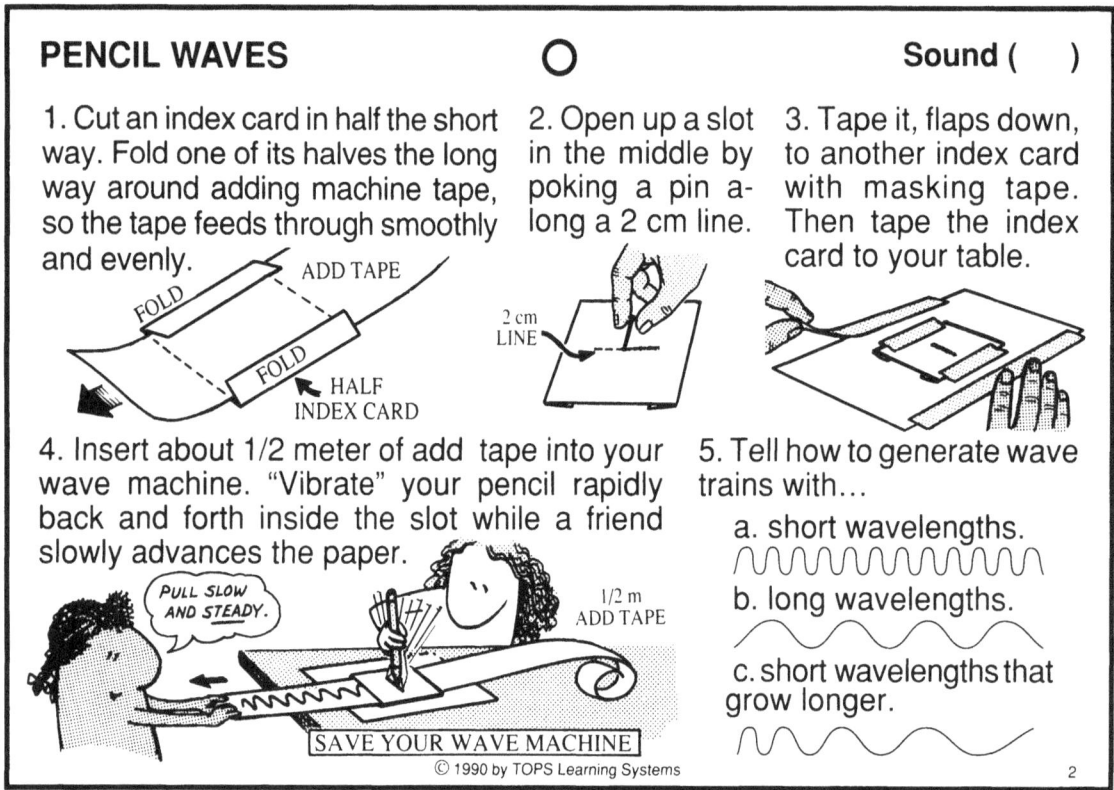

Answers / Notes

3. The flaps at each end must be kept free of masking tape so the adding machine tape will easily feed through in step 4.

5a. Short wavelengths are made by vibrating the pencil rapidly (and/or) by advancing the paper slowly.

5b. Long wavelengths are made by vibrating the pencil slowly (and/or) by advancing the paper rapidly.

5c. Short wavelengths that grow longer are made by slowing the rate of the vibrating pencil (and/or) by accelerating the advance of the paper.

The waves may look blocky because the pencil lead at the tip is the first to stop (at the end of the slot) and the last to start (in the reverse direction). Meanwhile the rest of the pencil (plus hand and arm that move it) stop and start more gradually. At faster paper speeds this pencil-point delay flattens the wave crests and troughs. And its rapid deceleration and acceleration steepen the slopes in between. The resulting wave pattern only approximates the normal sine curve.

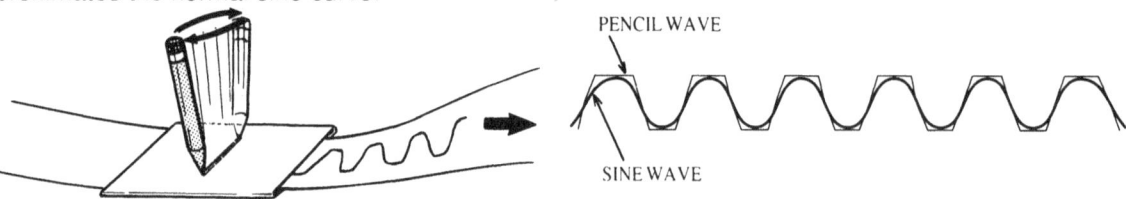

This squaring effect can be eliminated by lengthening the slot, then oscillating the pencil without touching the ends of the slot. The resulting wave train, though properly curved, no longer contains waves of uniform amplitude.

Materials

☐ Two 4x6 index cards.
☐ Scissors.
☐ Adding machine tape.
☐ A straight pin.
☐ Masking tape.

(TO) record the vibrating end of a bobby pin as a wave train by streaking it across greased glass.

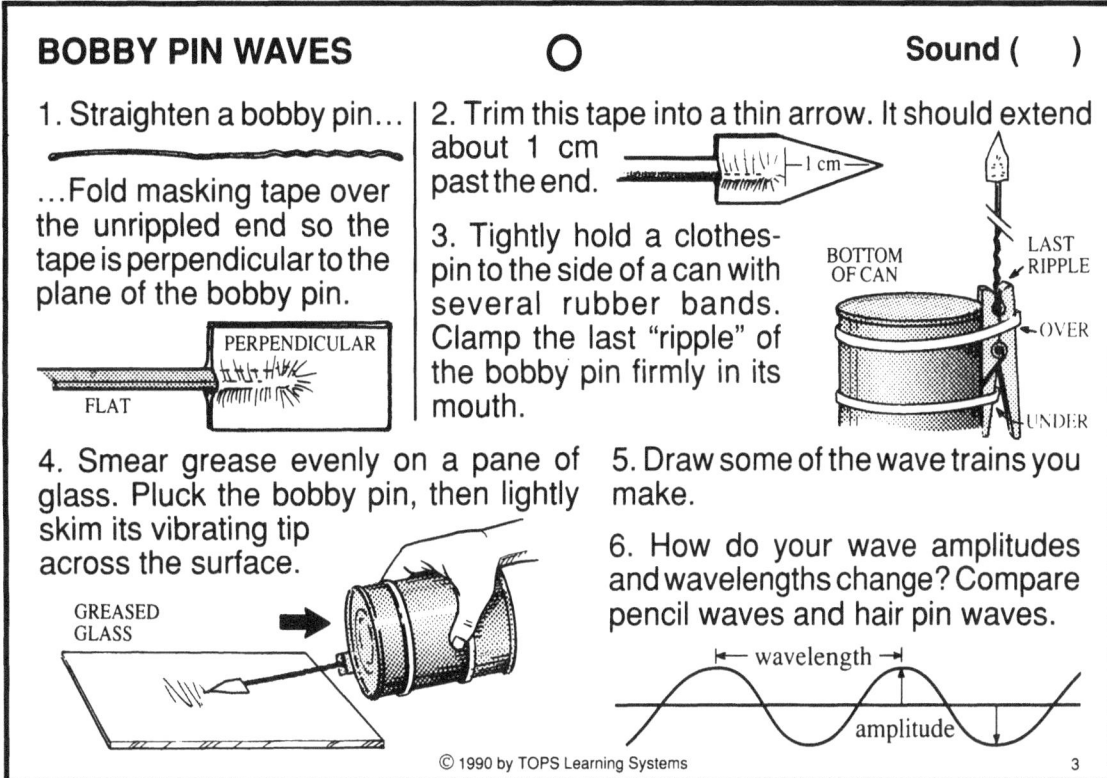

Introduction
Waves can be represented by sine curves. Amplitude refers to the distance from the midpoint of the wave to its high point (crest) or low point (trough). Wavelength is the distance between successive identical parts of the wave — from crest to crest, trough to trough, mid-point to mid-point, etc.

Answers / Notes
4. *To best observe the resulting wave trains, hold the glass pane up to a window or other strong light source to backlight the tracks.*

More dramatic effects can be obtained by drawing the vibrating arrow across glass smoked by a candle. But it is probably not worth the extra mess of wax and soot.

5.

SLOWER-MOVING TRAIN   FASTER-MOVING TRAIN

6. Wave amplitudes become progressively smaller over time (decay). Pencil waves, by contrast, maintained uniform amplitudes.

Wavelengths increased as the vibrating tip of the bobby pin is skimmed more rapidly over the grease, just as they did when paper was pulled more rapidly under the vibrating pencil.

Materials
- ☐ A bobby pin.
- ☐ Masking tape.
- ☐ Scissors.
- ☐ A clothespin.
- ☐ A medium-sized tin can.
- ☐ Rubber bands.
- ☐ Petroleum jelly.
- ☐ A pane of glass. Microscope slides can be substituted in a pinch, though they are really too small. Large hand mirrors are also suitable, though the wave trains cannot be seen quite as clearly.

(TO) measure frequency by counting cycles over measured units of time. To express frequency in cycles per second or Hertz units.

FREQUENCY O   Sound ( )

1. Hang a penny pendulum from your desk measuring 24.7 cm from its pivot to the center of the bob.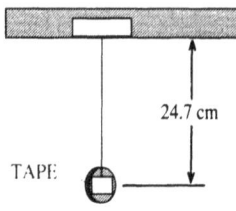

2. Your pendulum swings at a frequency of 1 Hertz. How many cycles per second equals 1 Hertz?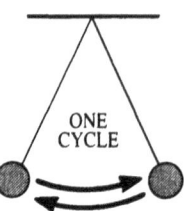

3. Measure your pulse rate. Express the frequency of your heart in Hertz units. Show your math.

4. Set up your wave machine with a protective strip of adding machine tape inside. Find your most natural frequency for vibrating the pencil.

a. Ask a friend to time you for 10 seconds while you count.   b. Fill in each trial until you get consistent results.

trial	1	2	3	4	5	6	7	8
cycles in 10 sec								
frequency (Hz)								

accepted natural frequency = ? Hz

© 1990 by TOPS Learning Systems

Answers / Notes

2. The pendulum ticks like a clock, completing 1 cycle each second. This implies that 1 Hertz is equivalent to 1 cycle per second.

3. Here is a sample calculation for a pulse of 72 beats per minute:

$$\frac{72 \text{ cycles}}{1 \text{ min}} \times \frac{1 \text{ min}}{60 \text{ sec}} = \frac{1.2 \text{ cycles}}{\text{sec}} = 1.2 \text{ Hz}$$

4b. *Emphasize that consistency is the main objective, not speed. If students move the pencil back and forth at a rate that feels comfortable and natural, they should be able to count the same number of cycles over each 10 second interval, give or take 2 cycles. Results typically fall within a range of 2 to 6 Hz. Here is one result:*

trial	1	2	3	4	5	6	7	8
cycles in 10 sec	48	46	50	48	47	49	48	
frequency (Hz)	4.8	4.6	5.0	4.8	4.7	4.9	4.8	

accepted natural frequency = 4.8 Hz

Materials

☐ A penny.
☐ Thread.
☐ Masking tape.
☐ A metric ruler. Use lab rulers or supply photocopies of the line master from the back of this book, plus scissors to cut out the ruler image.
☐ A wall clock with second-hand sweep. Or students can use their own wrist watches.
☐ The wave machine constructed in activity 1.
☐ Adding machine tape.

(TO) calculate the speed of a wave train, knowing its frequency.

WAVE TRAIN   ○   Sound ( )

1. Fix your wave machine to the table top with 1 m of add tape inside. Vibrate a pencil at your own natural frequency while a friend accelerates the tape from slow as a snail to fast as a fly.

2. Count the waves in your train, numbering every 5th wave at the crest.

3. Copy this table. Complete the first 2 columns, showing the total waves you made after each second.

4. Mark the passing of each second with a pencil mark on your tape. Measure the length of each one-second interval, then fill in the length and speed columns.

5. When was your wave train moving the slowest? Fastest? Find its average speed.

# of sec.	# of waves	each 1-second interval length (cm)	speed (cm/sec)
0	0	0	0
1			

© 1990 by TOPS Learning Systems

Introduction

Set up a wave machine. Demonstrate how to accelerate the adding machine tape through it, beginning at a snail's pace (perhaps 1 cm/sec) and ending as fast as a fly (perhaps 30 cm/sec).

Answers / Notes

3-4. *Answers will vary widely. This table is based on a natural pencil frequency of 4.8 Hz, experimentally determined in the previous activity.*

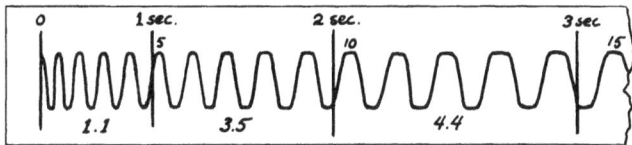

# of sec.	# of waves	each 1-second interval length (cm)	speed (cm/sec)
0	0	0	0
1	4.8	1.1	1.1
2	9.6	3.5	3.5
3	14.4	4.4	4.4
4	19.2	8.1	8.1
5	24.0	10.3	10.3
6	28.8	16.2	16.2
7	33.6	25.3	25.3
8	38.4	27.0	27.0

5. Analyzing the tape above, it moved slowest during the first second (1.1 cm/second); fastest during the final eighth second (27.0 cm/second). Overall, the wave train measured 96 cm and took 8 seconds to complete:

$$\text{Average speed} = \frac{96 \text{ cm}}{8 \text{ seconds}} = 12.0 \text{ cm/sec.}$$

Materials

☐ The wave machine constructed earlier.
☐ Adding machine tape.
☐ A metric ruler. Use a meter stick or photocopy the rulers on the supplementary page at the back of this book.
☐ A hand calculator (optional).

(TO) determine the speed that a tuning fork sweeps across greased glass, knowing the frequency of the wave train it leaves behind.

TUNING FORK WAVES Sound ( )

1. Get a tuning fork with the frequency stamped on it. Cut a thin arrow from masking tape. Fix it to the fork so the tip extends about 1.5 cm past an end.

2. Roughly estimate the speed (in cm/sec) that you can brush this arrow over the surface of a meter stick.

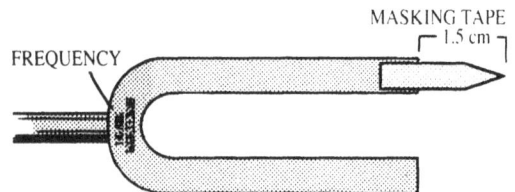

3. Now track the vibrating arrow over glass smeared with petroleum jelly and count the waves over a measured length. Calculate the speed of the arrow and compare it to your rough estimate.

Hint: speed = $\dfrac{cm}{sec}$ = $\dfrac{\cancel{cycle}}{sec} \times \dfrac{cm}{\cancel{cycle}}$

4. Repeat your analysis for a faster track. Find its speed in meters/sec.

© 1990 by TOPS Learning Systems

Answers / Notes

1. *Notice that the masking tape arrow is fixed to the bottom (or top) of the tuning fork, not to its side. In this position it flexibly bends in the vertical plane, making easy contact with the glass. But it remains rigid in the horizontal plane, enabling it to scrape a track through the grease as the fork vibrates back and forth.*

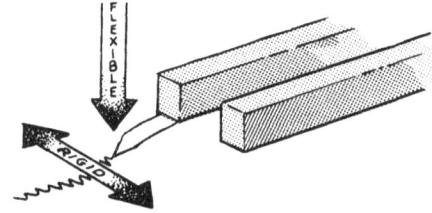

2-4. *Speeds will vary. Here are sample calculations for a 256 cycles/second tuning fork:*

• Estimated Speed:
The hand moves about 2 meters during a count of "a-thousand-one," or at a speed of 200 cm/sec.

• First Calculated Speed:
A train of 20 waves measures 10.8 cm.

$$\dfrac{256\ cyc}{sec} \times \dfrac{10.8\ cm}{20\ cyc} = \dfrac{138\ cm}{sec}$$

• Second Calculated Speed:
A train of 9 waves measures 7.1 cm.

$$\dfrac{256\ cyc}{sec} \times \dfrac{7.1\ cm}{9\ cyc} = \dfrac{202\ cm}{sec}$$

Students may be unfamiliar with speed units expressed as cm/sec. As an exercise in unit analysis, ask them to convert their speeds to more familiar kilometers/hour or miles/hour. Here is a sample conversion for 200 cm/sec.

$$\dfrac{200\ cm}{sec} \times \dfrac{60\ sec}{min} \times \dfrac{60\ min}{hr} = \dfrac{720{,}000\ cm}{hr}$$

$$\dfrac{720{,}000\ cm}{hr} \times \dfrac{m}{100\ cm} \times \dfrac{km}{1{,}000\ m} = \dfrac{7.2\ km}{hr}$$

$$\dfrac{7.2\ km}{hr} \times \dfrac{1\ mi}{1.6\ km} = \dfrac{4.5\ mi}{hr}$$

Materials

☐ A tuning fork of known frequency. Long, low-pitched tuning forks are easiest to use because they produce large sustained wave trains.
☐ Masking tape.
☐ Scissors.
☐ A meter stick or photocopied ruler.
☐ A pane of glass.
☐ Petroleum jelly.
☐ A hand calculator (optional).

(TO) understand that sound intensity increases with the amplitude of the vibrating source.

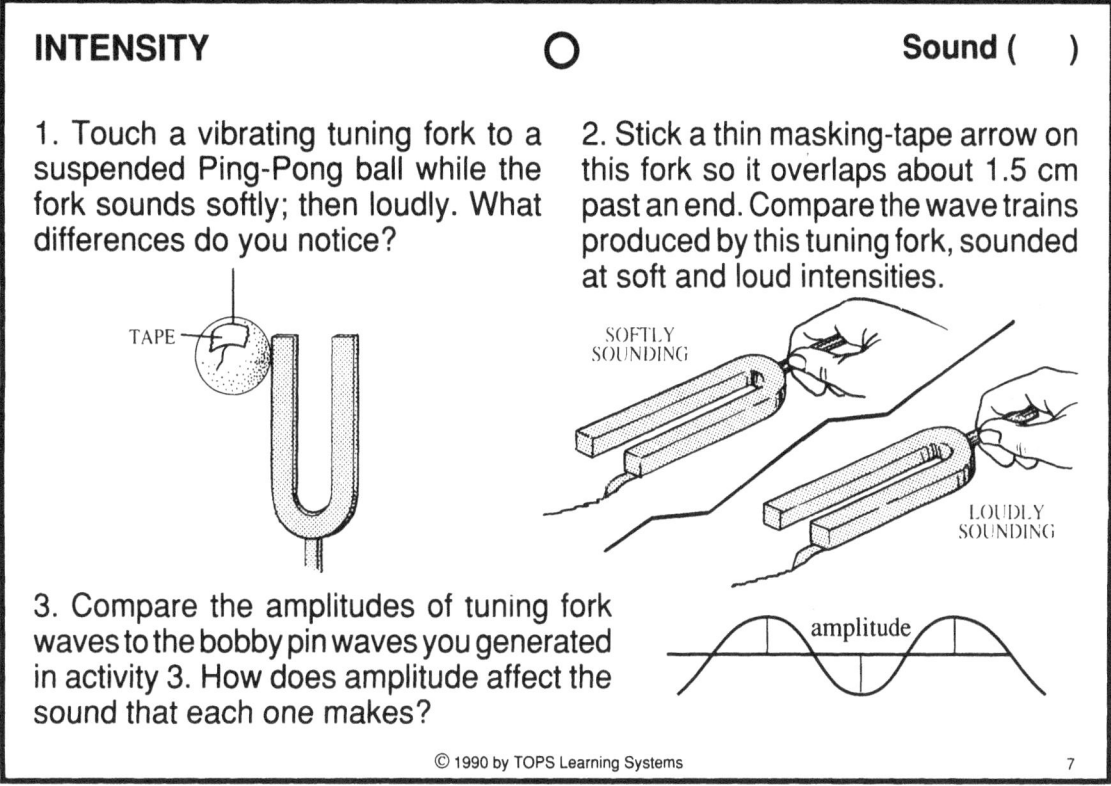

INTENSITY   ○   Sound ( )

1. Touch a vibrating tuning fork to a suspended Ping-Pong ball while the fork sounds softly; then loudly. What differences do you notice?

2. Stick a thin masking-tape arrow on this fork so it overlaps about 1.5 cm past an end. Compare the wave trains produced by this tuning fork, sounded at soft and loud intensities.

3. Compare the amplitudes of tuning fork waves to the bobby pin waves you generated in activity 3. How does amplitude affect the sound that each one makes?

© 1990 by TOPS Learning Systems

Answers / Notes

1. The ping pong ball is deflected through greater distances as the tuning fork is sounded at greater intensity.

2. Wave trains produced by a softly-sounding fork have lower amplitudes than those produced by the same fork sounded at higher intensity.

3. Tuning forks produce longer wave trains with sustained amplitudes. Hair pins produce shorter wave trains with rapidly decaying amplitudes.

Tuning-fork sounds, therefore, have a more constant intensity and longer duration. Bobby pins sound loudly at first, but their intensity fades rapidly.

Materials

- ☐ A tuning fork. Low-pitched forks work best.
- ☐ A Ping-Pong ball. A marble will also serve.
- ☐ Thread.
- ☐ Masking tape.
- ☐ Scissors.
- ☐ A pane of glass greased on the top surface.

(**TO**) appreciate that the pitch of a sound increases with the frequency of its vibrating source. To experimentally determine the ratio of frequencies for 2 tuning forks of different pitch.

PITCH Sound (   )

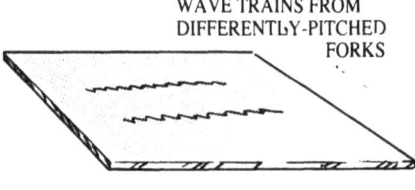
WAVE TRAINS FROM DIFFERENTLY-PITCHED FORKS

1. Make sound tracks for 2 tuning forks with different known pitches. Try to move each fork at about the same speed across the greased glass.

2. Diagram your results. How is the frequency at which a tuning fork vibrates related to the length of waves in its trains?

3. Strike the lower and higher pitched tuning forks so the arrows vibrate side by side. Ask a friend to brush greased glass under both vibrating arrows until you record 2 clear parallel tracks.

4. Count the waves in each track over any equal distance.

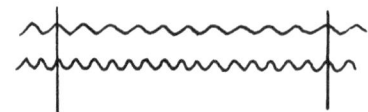

Compute these ratios. Are they equal?

$$\frac{\text{\# short waves}}{\text{\# long waves}} \stackrel{?}{=} \frac{\text{freq. high fork}}{\text{freq. low fork}}$$

© 1990 by TOPS Learning Systems

Answers / Notes

2. The higher-pitched fork produces wave trains with shorter wave lengths; the lower-pitched fork produces wave trains with longer wave lengths.

higher pitch: 〰〰〰
lower pitch: 〰〰

3. *Some practice and coordination is required to produce 2 clear wave trains. Stress how much easier it is to move 1 pane of glass under stationary tuning forks than to coordinate the movement of 2 tuning forks in 2 hands across stationary glass. In either case, the relative motion of vibrating masking tape over glass is the same.*

4. *Students should select any arbitrary distance, then count the number of waves in each track. The ratio of these two numbers should approximate the ratio of the known frequencies stamped on the tuning forks. This sample calculation is based on tuning forks with known frequencies of 440 c/s and 256 c/s.*

$$\frac{\text{\# short waves}}{\text{\# long waves}} = \frac{20}{12} = 1.67$$

$$\frac{\text{freq. high fork}}{\text{freq. low fork}} = \frac{440}{256} = 1.72$$

Allowing for experimental error, both ratios are the same.

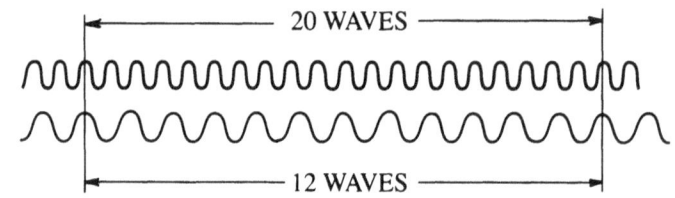

Materials

☐ Two tuning forks of known frequency.
☐ Masking tape.
☐ Scissors.
☐ A pane of glass greased on the top surface.
☐ A hand calculator (optional).

(TO) identify mediums of sound. To recognize that sound is transmitted as its medium vibrates.

SOUND MEDIUMS **Sound ( )**

1. Any material that carries sound is called a *sound medium*. List both the sound source and its medium in each experiment:

    a. Press your ear to a table top and tap on the surface with a pencil.
    b. Hold the handle of a vibrating tuning fork against your teeth or skull bones.
    c. Tie string to a fork. Hold the end of the string to your ear while dangling the fork against a table.
    d. Listen to a noise in the room.

SOURCE	MEDIUM
a.	
b.	
c.	
d.	

2. Line up 4 coins in a row and snap them with a fifth. Explain how these coins model atoms or molecules that carry sound in a medium.

3. Make a "telephone" from 2 cans and heavy string. Describe how sound travels from your vocal cords to a friend's eardrum.

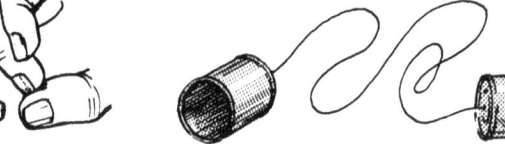

© 1990 by TOPS Learning Systems

Answers / Notes

1.

SOURCE	MEDIUM
a. pencil strikes a table	table top
b. vibrating tuning fork	teeth and bones in the head
c. vibrating dinner fork	string
d. (any noise source)	air

The vibrating dinner fork in step 1c transmits impressive chiming sounds up the string. Demonstrate, if necessary, how this string is pressed between a finger the outer ear, thereby covering the canal. There is no need to push the string inside the middle ear.

2. The fifth coin hits the fourth, which pushes against the third and so on, until the last coin is pushed off the end of the line. In a similar manner, vibrating molecules at the sound source bump into adjacent molecules in the sound medium, which in turn bump into other molecules and so on. This chain reaction propagates a vibration disturbance through the medium, which reaches our ears and is interpreted as sound.

3. The sender's vibrating vocal cords propagate a disturbance (sound wave) through the air. This disturbance vibrates the tin can. The can vibrates the string line. The string line vibrates the other tin can. It vibrates to send another disturbance (sound wave) through the air inside the can which, in turn, vibrates the receiver's ear drum.

Materials
☐ A tuning fork.
☐ A dinner fork. A spoon may be substituted. The resulting sound is still bell-like, though not as interesting.
☐ String. Heavy string works best. Don't substitute thread.
☐ Five pennies, or coins of other value.
☐ Two empty medium-sized tin cans with a nail hole punched into the bottom. If you wish students to perform this operation, supply a nail and hammer.

(TO) study differences between transverse and longitudinal waves.

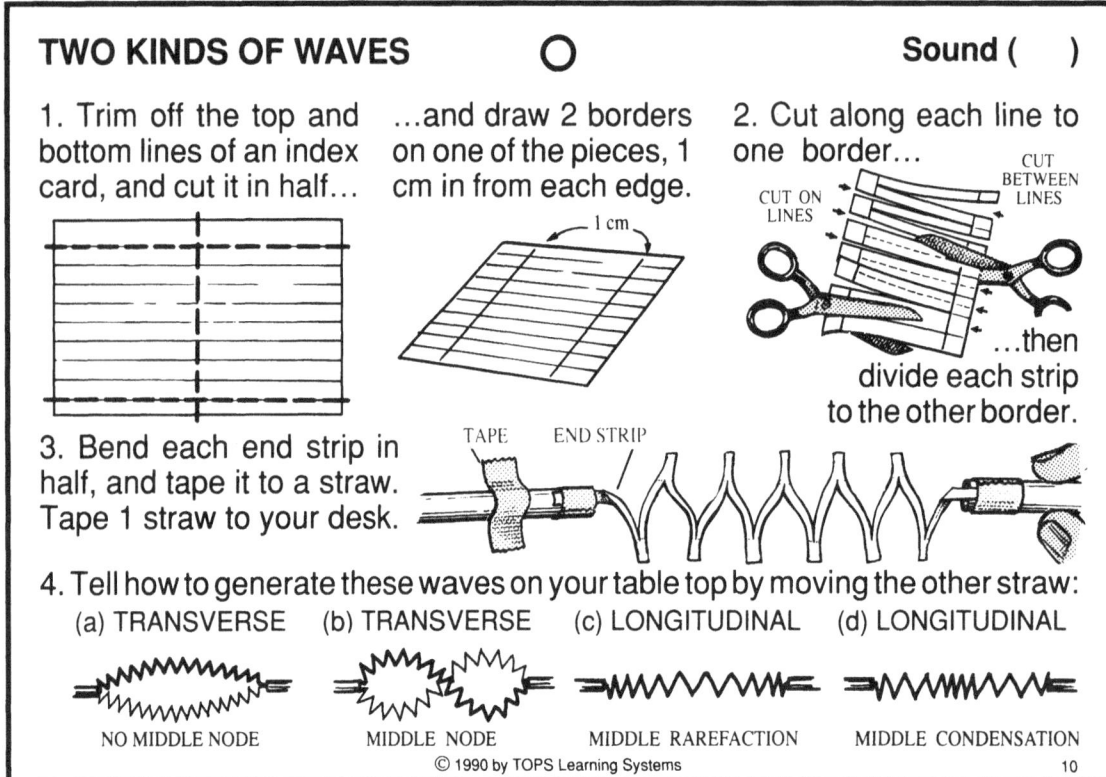

Answers / Notes

4a. Slowly move the straw that is not taped to the desk away from you and toward you, maintaining a uniform distance between both straws. *(The resulting transverse waves reflect back and forth, moving at right angles to the up and down motion of the paper coil.)*

4b. Rapidly move the same straw away from you and toward you, again maintaining a uniform distance between the straws.

4c. Slowly move this straw to the left and to the right, shrinking and expanding the distance between the straws. *(The resulting longitudinal wave reflects back and forth, moving parallel with the back and forth motion of the paper coil. This is easiest to observe if you displaced the straws over a relatively large distance.)*

4d. Rapidly move this straw to the left and to the right, again shrinking and expanding the distance between the straws. *(Instruct students to save their paper springs for the next activity.)*

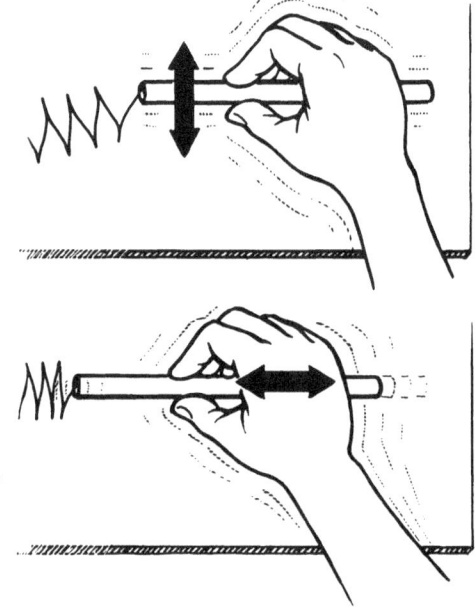

Materials
☐ A 4x6 index card.
☐ Scissors.
☐ Tape.
☐ Straight soda straws.

(TO) understand how longitudinal waves transmit sound energy.

LONGITUDINAL WAVES   Sound ( )

1. Set a can with both ends removed on clay supports. Hang index-card circles from narrow hinges of masking tape over each end. Make a smaller flap and a larger lid as shown.

2. Surround the can with your paper spring. Tape the end of each straw to the table.

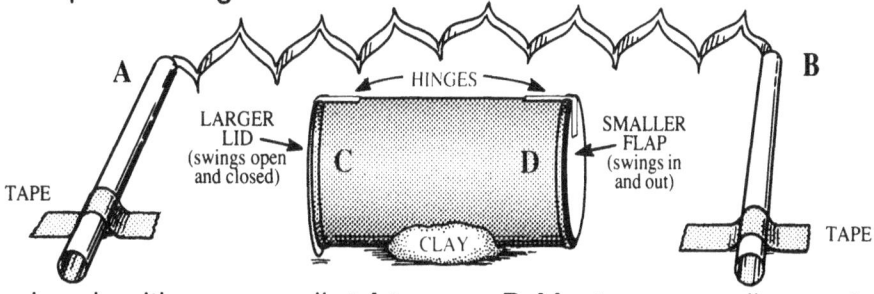

3. Tap sharply with your pencil at A to move B. Must a paper coil move the entire distance from A to B in order to transfer the energy across? Explain.

4. Tap lightly with your pencil at C to move D. Explain how squeezed-together air (a condensation) transfers energy through the can similar to a paper spring.

5. Quickly open the lid at C. Explain how stretched-apart air (a rarefaction) transfers energy to the flap at D.

6. Using dots to represent air molecules, draw how several sound waves might look as they move through the can.

© 1990 by TOPS Learning Systems

Answers / Notes

3. No. Each paper coil moves left, squeezing its neighbor only for an instant, and then relaxing to its original position. This squeeze (condensation) travels as a longitudinal wave from coil to coil through the entire spring, while each coil travels only a fraction of that distance.

4. Closing the lid at C pushes adjacent air molecules momentarily into neighboring molecules, that in turn push molecules next to them, and so on. A pulse of condensed air moves as a longitudinal wave through the entire can to D, even though individual air molecules move very little.

5. Opening the lid at C pulls air molecules out of the can. Adjacent air molecules rush in to fill the rarefaction or partial vacuum. These air molecules, in turn, leave space for still other molecules to fill. A pulse of rarefied air moves as a longitudinal wave through the entire can until it reaches the flap at D, which also moves inward.

6.
CONDENSATION

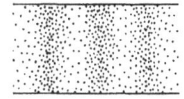

RAREFACTION

Materials

☐ A can with both ends removed.
☐ Modeling clay.
☐ An index card.
☐ Masking tape.
☐ Scissors.
☐ The paper spring constructed in the previous activity.

(TO) examine 3 ways to change the pitch of a vibrating string.

PITCH PROBLEM (1) Sound (   )

1. Push the end of some heavy string and light thread (about 1/2 m long) through a hole in the end of a can. Tie both strands to a paper clip.

2. Hold the can near your ear as you strum each strand. Experiment with different ways you can make high and low pitches.

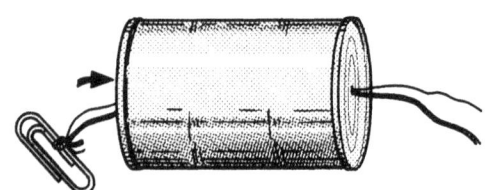 

3. Name 3 different variables that raise and lower the pitch of vibrating strings. Complete the table.

VARIABLE	To raise the pitch…	To lower the pitch…
a.		
b.		
c.		

4. As the pitch of a vibrating string is raised or lowered, what happens to its frequency?

© 1990 by TOPS Learning Systems

Answers / Notes

3.
VARIABLE	To raise the pitch…	To lower the pitch…
a. *tension*	…*increase it.*	…*decrease it.*
b. *length*	…*shorten it.*	…*lengthen it.*
c. *diameter*	…*use thinner string.*	…*use thicker string.*

4. As the pitch is lowered, the string vibrates at lower frequencies. As the pitch is raised, it vibrates at higher frequencies.

Materials
☐ A can with a nail hole punched in the end.
☐ Thread.
☐ Heavy string.
☐ A paper clip.

(TO) account for changes in pitch as water is added to a bottle. To identify 2 distinct sound sources.

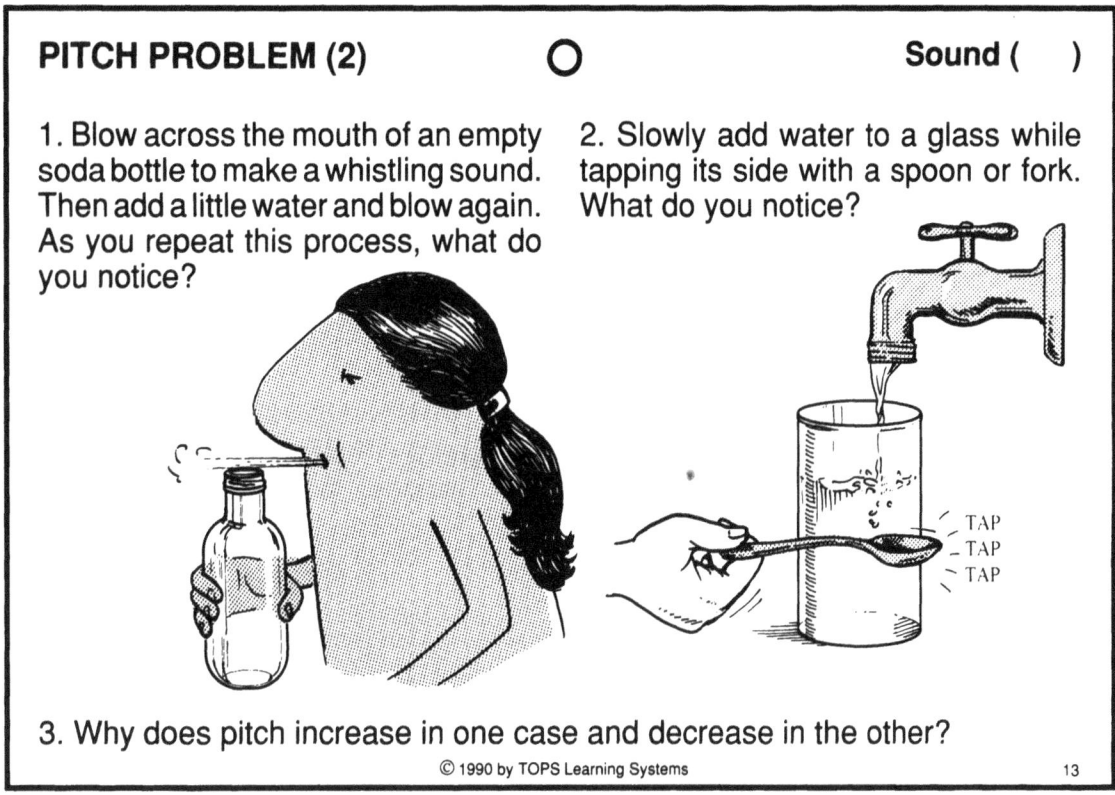

PITCH PROBLEM (2)   O   Sound ( )

1. Blow across the mouth of an empty soda bottle to make a whistling sound. Then add a little water and blow again. As you repeat this process, what do you notice?

2. Slowly add water to a glass while tapping its side with a spoon or fork. What do you notice?

3. Why does pitch increase in one case and decrease in the other?

© 1990 by TOPS Learning Systems

Answers / Notes

1. As the water level in the bottle rises, the pitch of the whistling sound becomes higher.

2. As the water level in the glass rises, the pitch of the tapping sound becomes lower.

3. The whistling sound in (1) is produced by a vibrating column of air inside the bottle. The rising water level shortens the air column, causing it to vibrate at higher and higher frequencies.

　　The tapping sound in (2) is produced by vibrating glass and water. Rising water in the glass increases its overall mass, causing it to vibrate at lower and lower frequencies.

Materials
☐ An empty soda bottle.
☐ A glass or beaker.
☐ A spoon or fork.

(TO) observe how objects with the same natural frequency resonate as one is sounded in the presence of the other.

RESANANCE

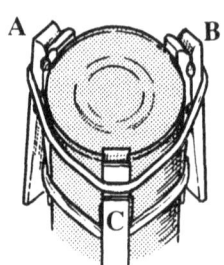 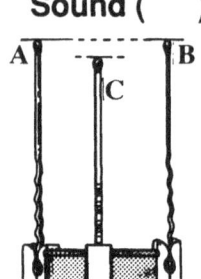

1. Tightly hold 3 clothespins to the bottom of a can with rubber bands. Label them A, B and C.

2. Unbend 3 bobby pins. Clamp 2 into A and B at the last "ripple" on the wavy end. Clamp the third into C at the next-to-the-last "ripple."

3. Measure all 3 pins to be sure A = B > C. Which pin sounds at the highest pitch? Which sound at the same pitch? Explain.

4. Strum each pin, 1 at a time, as you hold the can in your hand.

   a. Which pins resonate (vibrate together) even though you strum only one? Which don't?
   b. What do resonating pins have in common? Explain why this is so.

5. Adjust 2 soda bottles with water (if necessary) so they have the same pitch. While a friend blows a note on one bottle, hold the mouth of the second bottle first close to your ear, then away. What do you notice? Why?

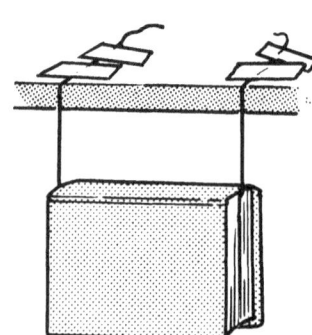

© 1990 by TOPS Learning Systems

Introduction

Hang a textbook from a loop of string that is firmly taped to the surface of your table. Challenge your class to make this book swing back and forth without pushing on it with any solid object. The solution is to blow on it, using puffs of air that are *sympathetic* to the natural frequency of the book pendulum. Little by little the book will swing higher and higher, swinging in *resonance* to the puffs of air that a student volunteer delivers. As this demonstration progresses, emphasize the new vocabulary.

Answers / Notes

3. Pin C sounds at the highest pitch. Having the shortest length, it vibrates at the highest frequency. Pins A and B sounds at the same pitch. Having the same length, they vibrate at the same frequency.

4a. Pins A and B tend to resonate. Strum one, and the other vibrates as well. Pin C, by contrast, vibrates alone, resonating very little with A or B.

4b. Pins that resonate together have the same length, and thus the same frequency of vibration. Vibrating the first delivers energy pulses through the can that exactly match the frequency of the second. This causes both to vibrate, the second resonating in sympathy with the first. (*If you hold the can firmly to the table, so it cannot vibrate, the pins will not resonate. This demonstrates that the sympathetic vibrations are transferred through the can and not through the air as in step 5.*)

5. The air in the second bottle tends to amplify the note played on the first. Since it sounds the same note, it has a column of air that vibrates at the same frequency. Thus it resonates with the first to reinforce the sound.

Materials

☐ Clothespins.
☐ A medium-sized can.
☐ Rubber bands and bobby pins.
☐ A ruler. Use your own lab rulers, or a photocopy from the back of this book.
☐ Soda bottles.

(TO) hear beats between interacting tones with slightly different pitches. To understand why the beat frequency decreases as tones converge to the same pitch.

BEATS   ○   Sound ( )

1. Cut out all 5 frequency strips. If each line represents a wave crest, and each number counts a second, write the frequency (in Hertz) at the top of each strip.
2. Rub oil on each strip so the paper becomes semi-transparent.
3. Press these strips together (2 at a time) so the seconds line up. Hold up the paper to good light to observe how the wave trains *beat* (bunch and spread).
   a. Fill in the table: count the beats/second between each pair of strips.
   b. What mathematical regularity can you discover?

	8 Hz	9 Hz	10 Hz	12 Hz
8 Hz	b/s	b/s	b/s	b/s
9 Hz			b/s	b/s
10 Hz				b/s

4. Layer together 6 pieces of masking tape about finger length:
5. Get 2 tuning forks of equal frequency (or 1 octave apart). Cut narrow pads of tape to attach to *one* of the forks. PAD ALL SURFACES

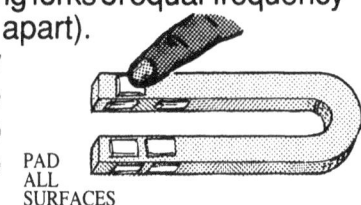

6. Strike both forks. Hold them near an ear like this and listen to the beats.

7. How does the frequency of these beats change as you remove pads of tape? Use your results from step 3 to explain your observations.

© 1990 by TOPS Learning Systems

Answers / Notes

1. The strips have these frequencies: 8 Hz, 8 Hz, 9 Hz, 10 Hz and 12 Hz.

3a.

	8 Hz	9 Hz	10 Hz	12 Hz
8 Hz	0 b/s	1 b/s	2 b/s	4 b/s
9 Hz			1 b/s	3 b/s
10 Hz				2 b/s

3b. The beat frequency equals the frequency difference between 2 interacting wave trains.

7. As the pads of tape are removed, the frequency of the beats decreases (slows down). Removing masking tape makes that fork vibrate at a slightly higher frequency, closer to the pitch of the fork that is not taped. As these two frequencies converge to the same pitch, their difference, the beat frequency, approaches zero.

Materials
☐ Five frequency strips. Photocopy these from the supplementary page at the back of this book, 1 set per lab group.
☐ Cooking oil or baby oil.
☐ Masking tape.
☐ Scissors.
☐ Two tuning forks of equal frequency. Forks that are 1 octave apart also work.

(TO) investigate the mathematical relationship between vibrating wires that sound octaves apart.

OCTAVE RULES   Sound ( )

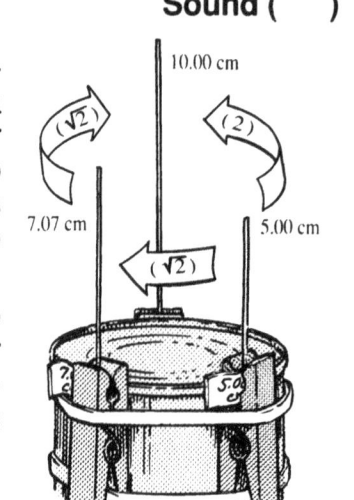

1. Flag 3 pieces of wire with masking tape that accurately measures each length.

2. Tightly hold 3 clothespins to the bottom of a can with several rubber bands. Clamp a wire into each clothespin so its measured length is free to vibrate.

3. Strum each wire while holding the can to your ear. What is the relationship between its length and its pitch?

4. Adjust 3 more untagged wires so they sound 1 octave apart. Confirm that the ratio of their lengths is close to the predicted values.

5. Each new higher octave vibrates at twice the frequency of the previous lower octave. If middle C vibrates at 256 Hz., what is the frequency of...
   a. high C.   b. low C.
   c. one octave below low C.

© 1990 by TOPS Learning Systems

Introduction
Demonstrate octaves. Sound a note on a tuning fork, asking your class to hum one octave above and below.

Answers / Notes
3. Wires that sound ONE octave apart are related by $\sqrt{2}$: the shorter divides into the longer $\sqrt{2}$ times. Or, the shorter multiplied by $\sqrt{2}$ equals the longer.

Wires that sound TWO octaves apart are related by the whole number 2: the shorter divides twice into the longer. Or, twice the shorter equals the longer.

4. Students should select wires that sound within their ability to discern pitch. Those who are tone deaf will need assistance. Here is one result:

$$\frac{6.75}{4.70} = 1.44 \approx \sqrt{2} \quad \frac{4.70}{3.30} = 1.42 \approx \sqrt{2} \quad \frac{6.75}{3.30} = 2.04 \approx 2$$

5. *Here students explore the relationship between pitch and FREQUENCY. Point out that this is a new and separate rule, different from the rule already established about pitch and wire LENGTH.*

high C = 2 x 256 Hz = 512 Hz
low C = 1/2 x 256 Hz = 128 Hz
one octave below low C = 1/2 x 128 Hz = 64 Hz

Materials
☐ Thin wire. The results in this activity are based on 22 gauge galvanized iron wire.
☐ Wire cutters. You might also break the wire by rapidly bending it back and forth.
☐ Masking tape.
☐ A medium-sized can.
☐ Clothespins.
☐ Rubber bands.
☐ A metric ruler. The paper ruler photocopied from the back of this book can be used with some advantage. It is thin enough to slip between the jaws of the clothespin in step 4, so each wire's length can be measured from the point where it is actually clamped.
☐ A hand calculator (optional).

(TO) confirm the octave rules for long vibrating wire. To explore the lower threshold of sound.

HOW LOW CAN YOU GO? ○   Sound ( )

1. Adjust a wire to sound at middle C (256 Hz). Accurately measure the length of the part that is free to vibrate.

2. Repeat 2 more times. Choose your most consistent result or find an average.

Trial	Length (cm)
1	
2	
3	

3. Apply this result plus your octave rules to complete this table.

frequency (Hz)	256	128	64	32	16	8	4	2	1
length (cm)									

4. At what frequency does the wire vibrate too slowly to hear? (What is your lower threshold of hearing?)

5. Measure out enough wire to vibrate at 1 Hz. Confirm that it really does.

© 1990 by TOPS Learning Systems

Answers / Notes

1. A length of 4.19 cm was obtained for 22 gauge galvanized iron wire. Other kinds of wire with other thicknesses will yield different results.

Students should begin measuring where the wire is actually clamped to the clothespin. The photocopied ruler works best in this application because it is thin enough to fit the narrow space, and has a zero point that is flush with the bottom.

2.
Trial	Length (cm)
1	4.17
2	4.20
3	4.19

average = 4.19

Repeating this measurement 3 times assures greater accuracy. Measuring error that remains will be multiplied up to a factor of 16 in the next step.

3.
frequency (Hz)	256	128	64	32	16	8	4	2	1
length (cm)	4.19	5.92	8.38	11.84	16.76	23.68	33.52	47.36	67.04

The first length in this table comes from step 2. Multiply that by 1.41 to find the second. Because the pitch lowers 2 octaves each time the wire's length is doubled, simply double these first two entries, alternating between them, to complete the rest of the table.

4. A 32 Hz vibration sounds very soft and very low. A 16 Hz vibration is silent except for background noise associated with plucking the wire. The lower threshold of human hearing, therefore, lies between 32 and 16 Hz.

Caution students not to confuse this low fundamental tone with much higher tones that sound whenever the wire is merely touched. These higher tones are associated with longitudinal vibrations that run throughout the wire. They can be minimized by "leaning" a finger against the wire, then withdrawing it quickly in the same direction that the wire will move into its first vibration.

5. *Students should measure out the predicted length of wire and confirm that it "ticks" with a frequency of 1 Hz, completing 1 full cycle each new second.*

Materials

☐ A can, clothespin and rubber bands.
☐ Thin wire, as used previously.
☐ A metric ruler.
☐ A hand calculator (optional).
☐ A middle C tuning fork (256 Hz). A higher or lower octave may be substituted.

(TO) build a working model of a phonograph. To understand how it works.

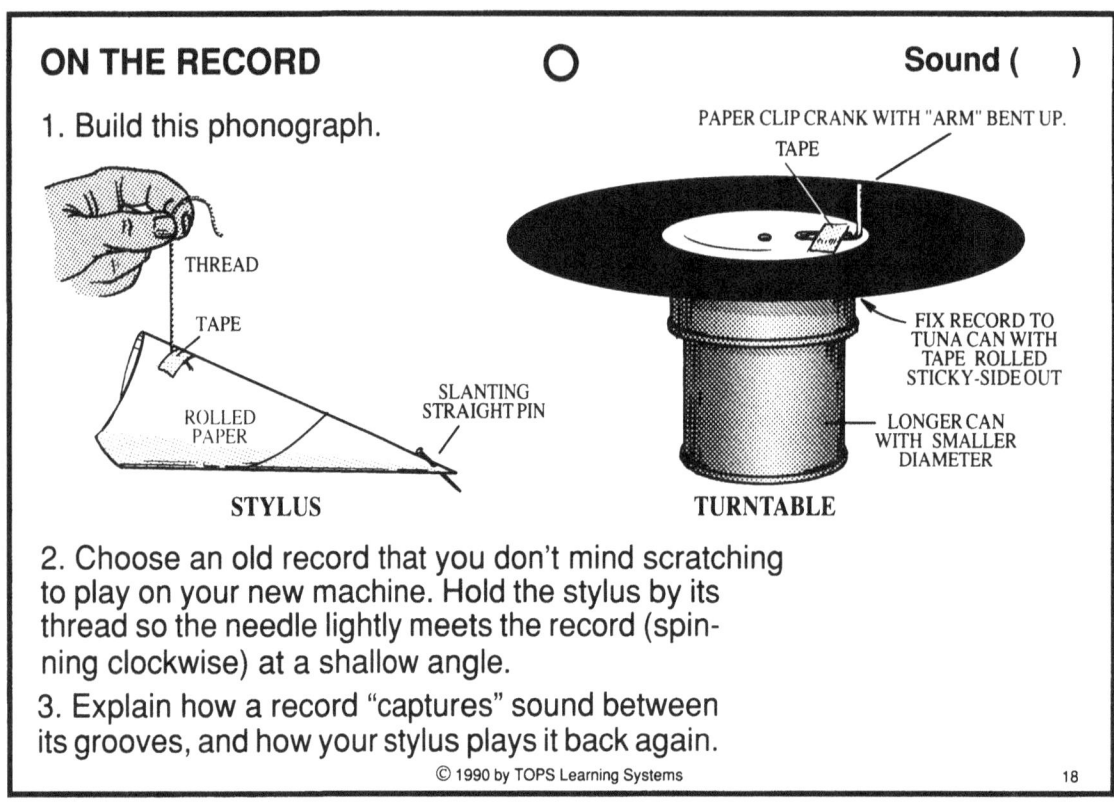

Answers / Notes

2. The "music" has low fidelity to be sure, but can still be recognized if the record is turned with reasonably constant RPM somewhere near its proper recording speed. If students fail to produce recognized sounds, try spinning the record on a commercial turntable, using only the improvised stylus to reproduce the sound. The paper cone and pin will amplify the recording with amazing clarity.

3. Sound vibrations are recorded between the record grooves as a series of waves, similar to those recorded by the tuning fork skimmed across greased glass. As the stylus pin moves over these waves, it vibrates just like the original sound. These vibrations are greatly amplified by the paper cone and transmitted through the air as longitudinal sound waves.

Materials

- ☐ A medium-sized can.
- ☐ A short tunafish can, or equivalent, that fits over the longer can and turns easily without too much wobble.
- ☐ Masking tape.
- ☐ An old phonograph record.
- ☐ A paper clip.
- ☐ A piece of scratch paper.
- ☐ A straight pin.
- ☐ Thread.

(TO) build a reed instrument. To experiment with variables that change the pitch.

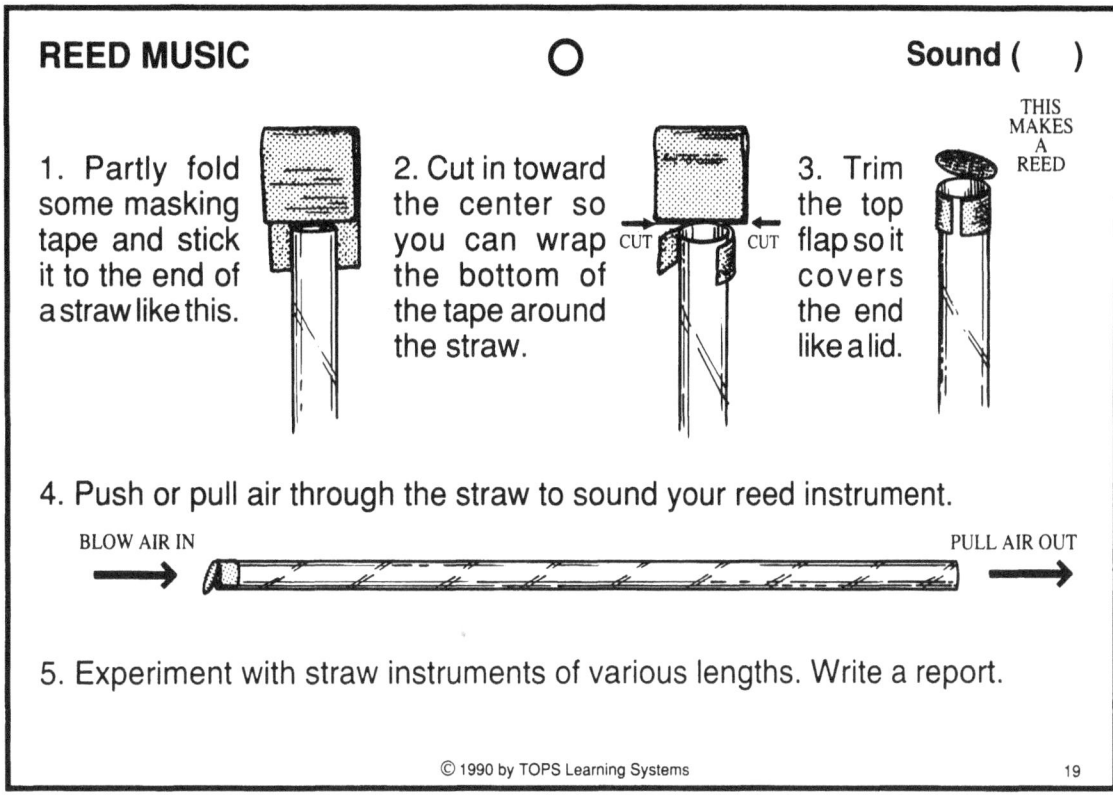

Answers / Notes

5. *To conserve straws, you might recommend that students experiment with these components:*

1 Sounder: Cut a straw in half; attach a reed.

1 Slider: Cut a straw in half; cut open along its length and slide over a whole straw; tape along its entire length.

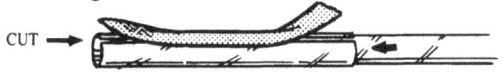

3 Extensions: Use uncut whole straws.

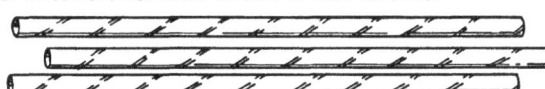

3 Connectors: Cut short segments of straw twice the width of masking tape; cut each open along its length and slide over a whole straw; tape only the center.

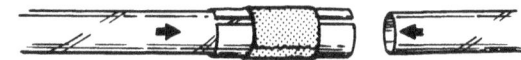

1 Finger Board: Cut finger holes in a whole straw by pinching half holes along the side with a paper punch.

REPORT:

• Sound is produced by blowing on the masking tape reed to make it vibrate. This, in turn, vibrates a column of air inside in the straw. The longer the straw, the longer the vibrating column of air, the lower its frequency, the lower its pitch.
• The straw is a bass instrument. Three straws connected to a sounder produce an astonishingly low note. A half straw sounds in the medium register. Straws shorter than 1/2 straw don't sound at all.
• The vibrating column of air may be changed more rapidly by opening and closing holes on the finger board (like a clarinet), or by moving the slider in and out (like a trombone).

Materials

☐ Straight straws.   ☐ Scissors.
☐ Masking tape.   ☐ A paper punch.

(TO) experimentally calculate the speed of sound in air.

SPEED OF SOUND Sound ( )

1. Stand far enough from a wall or building so you can hear a distinct echo when clapping wood blocks together.

2. Clap these blocks just fast enough so the returning echo is totally drowned out by the sound of the next clap. Measure this frequency in claps/minute.

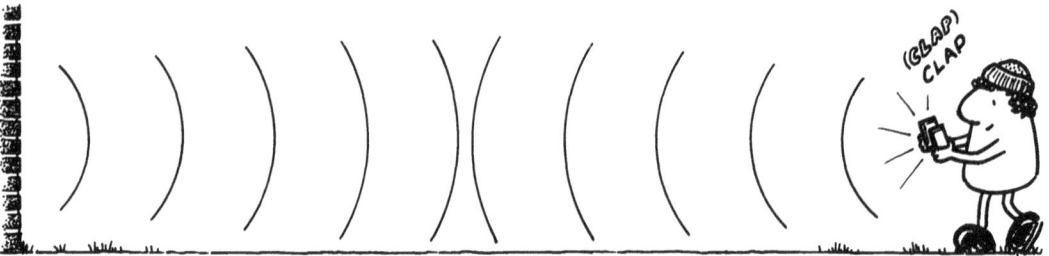

3. Measure how far the sound travels (to the wall and back) to reach your ear.

4. Calculate the speed of sound through air in meters per second.

$$\frac{\text{meters}}{\text{sec}} = \frac{\text{meters}}{\text{clap}} \times \frac{\text{claps}}{\text{min}} \times \frac{\text{min}}{\text{sec}}$$

© 1990 by TOPS Learning Systems

Answers / Notes

Here is a model calculation. At a distance of 50 meters from a building it is necessary to clap the boards together about 200 claps/minute to mask the sound of the returning echoes. This means that after the boards are clapped together once, sound travels 50 meters to the building, plus 50 meters back to the observer, before the boards are clapped again.

$$\frac{100 \text{ meters}}{\text{clap}} \times \frac{200 \text{ claps}}{\text{minutes}} \times \frac{1 \text{ minute}}{60 \text{ seconds}} = \frac{333 \text{ meters}}{\text{second}}$$

The speed of sound in air varies somewhat with temperature and humidity. In dry air at 0° C it travels about 330 meters per second. At normal room temperature or 20° C, sound travels about 340 m/s.

Discussion

If there is a 5-second delay between a flash of lightning and the sound of thunder, how far away did the lightning flash? (Assume the full 5 seconds is used for sound travel, since light arrives instantaneously over short distances.) Here is a calculation in miles:

$$\frac{333 \text{ meters}}{\text{second}} \times \frac{1 \text{ kilometer}}{1000 \text{ meters}} \times \frac{1 \text{ mile}}{1.6 \text{ kilometers}} \times \frac{5 \text{ seconds}}{1} \approx 1 \text{ mile}$$

Materials

☐ Any large flat structure (a wall or side of a building) that borders on a field or large open area.
☐ A watch with a second hand
☐ A meter stick or measuring tape.
☐ Wood blocks. A spoon and pan also produce sharp distinct echoes.

REPRODUCIBLE STUDENT TASK CARDS

These Reproducible Student Task Cards may be duplicated for use with this module only, provided such reproductions bear copyright notice. Beyond single-classroom use, reproduction of these task cards by schools or school systems for wider dissemination, or by anyone for commercial sale, is strictly prohibited.

Task Cards Options

Here are 3 management options to consider before you photocopy:

1. Consumable Worksheets: Copy 1 complete set of task card pages. Cut out each card and fix it to a separate sheet of boldly lined paper. Duplicate a class set of each worksheet master you have made, 1 per student. Direct students to follow the task card instructions at the top of each page, then respond to questions in the lined space underneath.

2. Nonconsumable Reference Booklets: Copy and collate the 2-up task card pages in sequence. Make perhaps half as many sets as the students who will use them. Staple each set in the upper left corner, both front and back to prevent the outside pages from working loose. Tell students that these task card booklets are for reference only. They should use them as they would any textbook, responding to questions on their own papers, returning them unmarked and in good shape at the end of the module.

3. Nonconsumable Task Cards: Copy several sets of task card pages. Laminate them, if you wish, for extra durability, then cut out each card to display in your room. You might pin cards to bulletin boards; or punch out the holes and hang them from wall hooks (you can fashion hooks from paper clips and tape these to the wall); or fix cards to cereal boxes with paper fasteners, 4 to a box; or keep cards on designated reference tables. The important thing is to provide enough task card reference points about your classroom to avoid a jam of too many students at any one location. Two or 3 task card sets should accommodate everyone, since different students will use different cards at different times.

SOURCES OF SOUND Sound ( )

1. Do each experiment and write what you observe:

   a. Strike a tuning fork. While it is still humming, place the end in a glass of water.

   b. Straighten a bobby pin. Hold it against an inverted can while you strum the end.

   c. Touch your Adam's apple as you intermittently hum a low note.

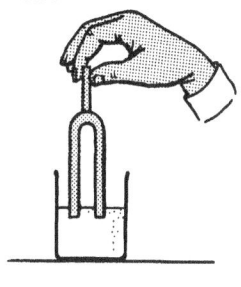 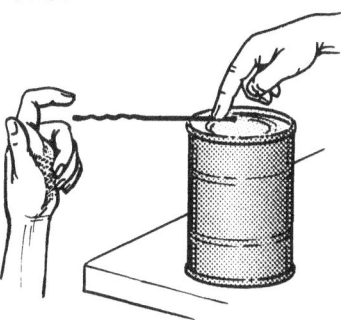 

2. What do tuning forks, hair pins, and vocal cords all do in order to produce sound?

3. Blow across the top of a soda bottle to make a note; tap on it with scissors. What vibrates to produce each sound?

© 1990 by TOPS Learning Systems

1

PENCIL WAVES Sound ( )

1. Cut an index card in half the short way. Fold one of its halves the long way around adding machine tape, so the tape feeds through smoothly and evenly.

2. Open up a slot in the middle by poking a pin along a 2 cm line.

3. Tape it, flaps down, to another index card with masking tape. Then tape the index card to your table.

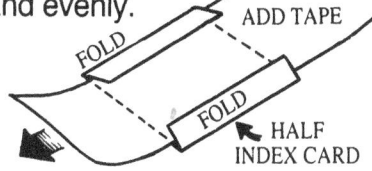 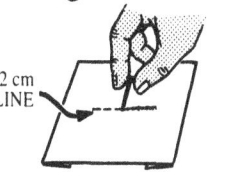 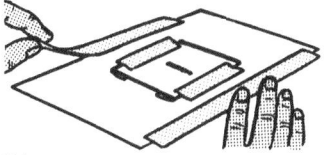

4. Insert about 1/2 meter of add tape into your wave machine. "Vibrate" your pencil rapidly back and forth inside the slot while a friend slowly advances the paper.

5. Tell how to generate wave trains with...

   a. short wavelengths.

   b. long wavelengths.

   c. short wavelengths that grow longer.

© 1990 by TOPS Learning Systems

2

cards 1-2

BOBBY PIN WAVES Sound ( )

1. Straighten a bobby pin...

...Fold masking tape over the unrippled end so the tape is perpendicular to the plane of the bobby pin.

2. Trim this tape into a thin arrow. It should extend about 1 cm past the end.

3. Tightly hold a clothespin to the side of a can with several rubber bands. Clamp the last "ripple" of the bobby pin firmly in its mouth.

4. Smear grease evenly on a pane of glass. Pluck the bobby pin, then lightly skim its vibrating tip across the surface.

5. Draw some of the wave trains you make.

6. How do your wave amplitudes and wavelengths change? Compare pencil waves and hair pin waves.

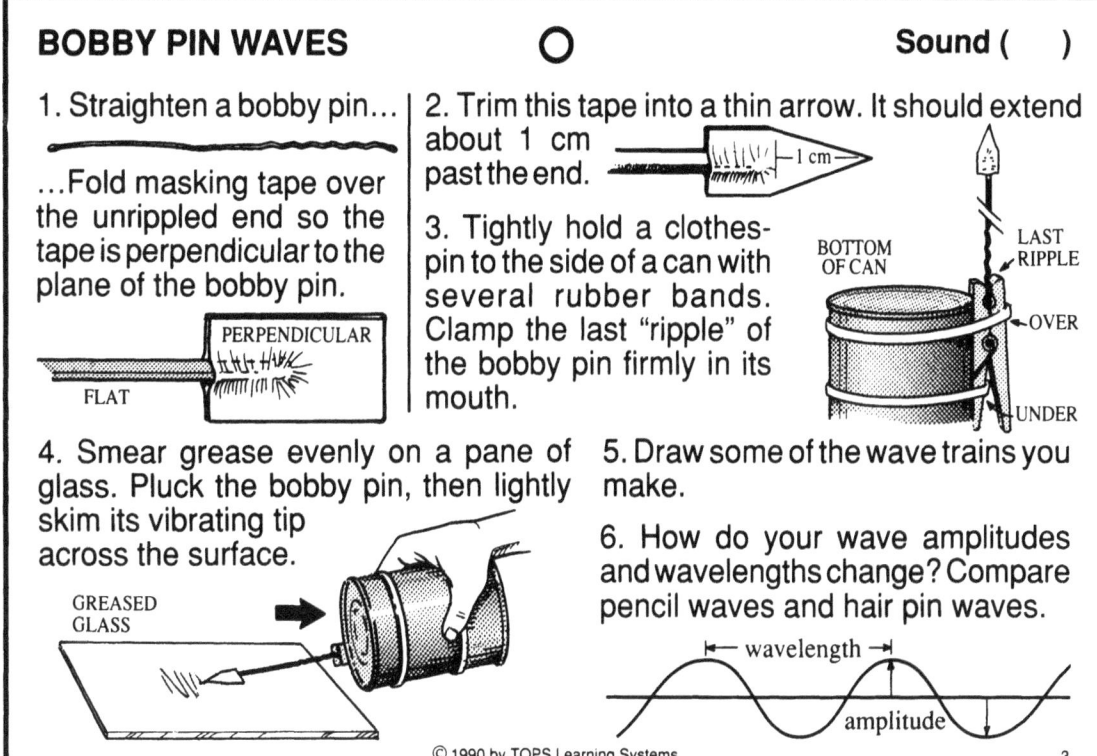

FREQUENCY Sound ( )

1. Hang a penny pendulum from your desk measuring 24.7 cm from its pivot to the center of the bob.

2. Your pendulum swings at a frequency of 1 Hertz. How many cycles per second equals 1 Hertz?

3. Measure your pulse rate. Express the frequency of your heart in Hertz units. Show your math.

4. Set up your wave machine with a protective strip of adding machine tape inside. Find your most natural frequency for vibrating the pencil.

   a. Ask a friend to time you for 10 seconds while you count.

   b. Fill in each trial until you get consistent results.

trial	1	2	3	4	5	6	7	8
cycles in 10 sec								
frequency (Hz)								

accepted natural frequency = ? Hz

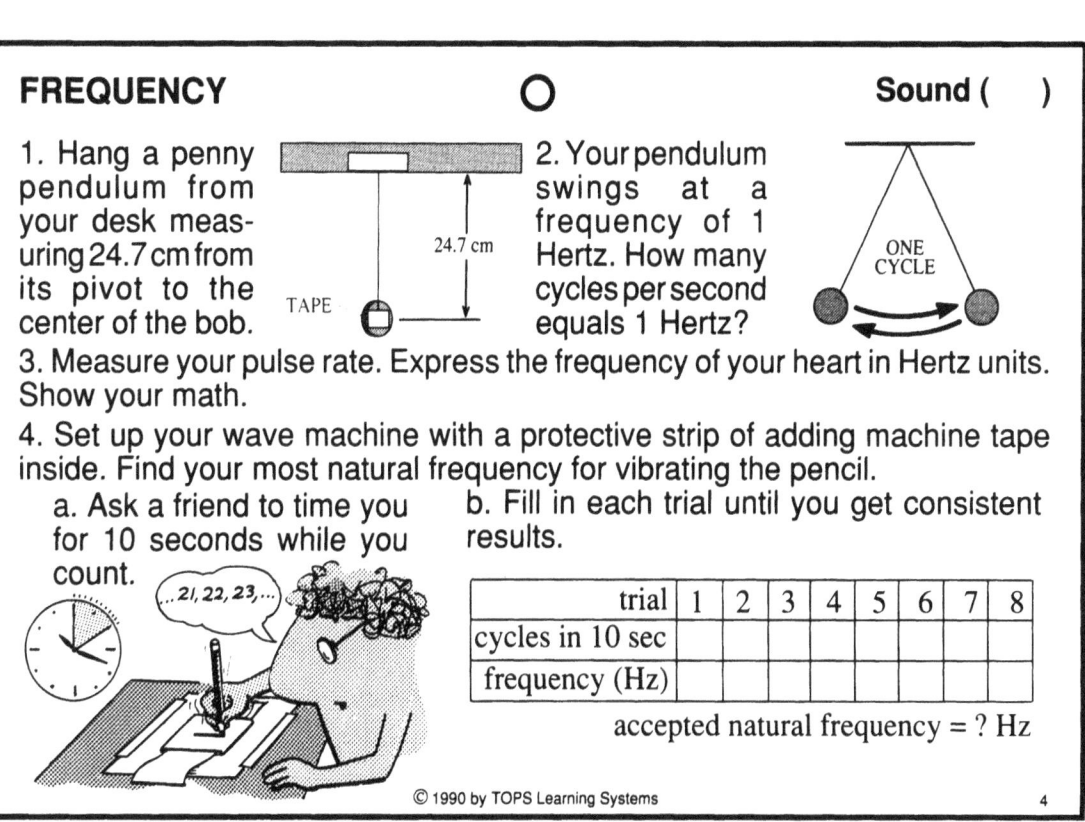

WAVE TRAIN   Sound (   )

1. Fix your wave machine to the table top with 1 m of add tape inside. Vibrate a pencil at your own natural frequency while a friend accelerates the tape from slow as a snail to fast as a fly.

2. Count the waves in your train, numbering every 5th wave at the crest.

3. Copy this table. Complete the first 2 columns, showing the total waves you made after each second.

4. Mark the passing of each second with a pencil mark on your tape. Measure the length of each one-second interval, then fill in the length and speed columns.

5. When was your wave train moving the slowest? Fastest? Find its average speed.

# of sec.	# of waves	each 1-second interval length (cm)	speed (cm/sec)
0	0	0	0
1			

© 1990 by TOPS Learning Systems

TUNING FORK WAVES   Sound (   )

1. Get a tuning fork with the frequency stamped on it. Cut a thin arrow from masking tape. Fix it to the fork so the tip extends about 1.5 cm past an end.

2. Roughly estimate the speed (in cm/sec) that you can brush this arrow over the surface of a meter stick.

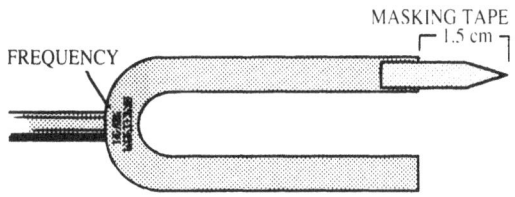

3. Now track the vibrating arrow over glass smeared with petroleum jelly and count the waves over a measured length. Calculate the speed of the arrow and compare it to your rough estimate.

Hint: speed $= \dfrac{cm}{sec} = \dfrac{\cancel{cycle}}{sec} \times \dfrac{cm}{\cancel{cycle}}$

4. Repeat your analysis for a faster track. Find its speed in meters/sec.

© 1990 by TOPS Learning Systems

INTENSITY ○ Sound ( )

1. Touch a vibrating tuning fork to a suspended Ping-Pong ball while the fork sounds softly; then loudly. What differences do you notice?

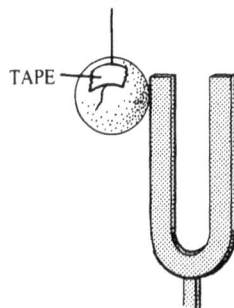

2. Stick a thin masking-tape arrow on this fork so it overlaps about 1.5 cm past an end. Compare the wave trains produced by this tuning fork, sounded at soft and loud intensities.

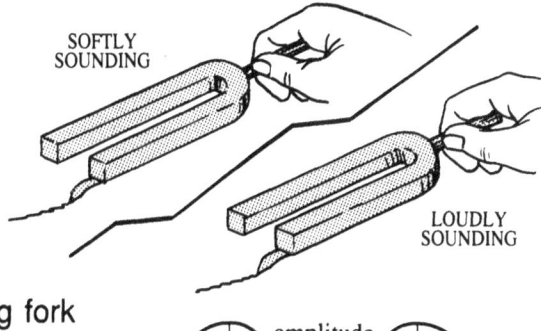

3. Compare the amplitudes of tuning fork waves to the bobby pin waves you generated in activity 3. How does amplitude affect the sound that each one makes?

© 1990 by TOPS Learning Systems

PITCH ○ Sound ( )

1. Make sound tracks for 2 tuning forks with different known pitches. Try to move each fork at about the same speed across the greased glass.

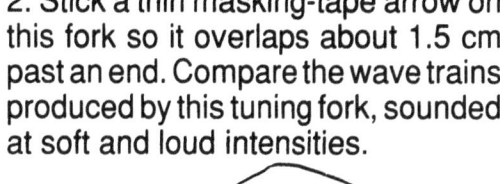
WAVE TRAINS FROM DIFFERENTLY-PITCHED FORKS

2. Diagram your results. How is the frequency at which a tuning fork vibrates related to the length of waves in its trains?

3. Strike the lower and higher pitched tuning forks so the arrows vibrate side by side. Ask a friend to brush greased glass under both vibrating arrows until you record 2 clear parallel tracks.

4. Count the waves in each track over any equal distance.

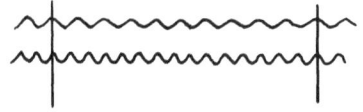

Compute these ratios. Are they equal?

$$\frac{\text{\# short waves}}{\text{\# long waves}} \stackrel{?}{=} \frac{\text{freq. high fork}}{\text{freq. low fork}}$$

© 1990 by TOPS Learning Systems

SOUND MEDIUMS ○ Sound ( )

1. Any material that carries sound is called a *sound medium*. List both the sound source and its medium in each experiment:
   a. Press your ear to a table top and tap on the surface with a pencil.
   b. Hold the handle of a vibrating tuning fork against your teeth or skull bones.
   c. Tie string to a fork. Hold the end of the string to your ear while dangling the fork against a table.
   d. Listen to a noise in the room.

SOURCE	MEDIUM
a.	
b.	
c.	
d.	

2. Line up 4 coins in a row and snap them with a fifth. Explain how these coins model atoms or molecules that carry sound in a medium.

3. Make a "telephone" from 2 cans and heavy string. Describe how sound travels from your vocal cords to a friend's eardrum.

© 1990 by TOPS Learning Systems

TWO KINDS OF WAVES ○ Sound ( )

1. Trim off the top and bottom lines of an index card, and cut it in half... ...and draw 2 borders on one of the pieces, 1 cm in from each edge.

2. Cut along each line to one border...

...then divide each strip to the other border.

3. Bend each end strip in half, and tape it to a straw. Tape 1 straw to your desk.

4. Tell how to generate these waves on your table top by moving the other straw:
   (a) TRANSVERSE (b) TRANSVERSE (c) LONGITUDINAL (d) LONGITUDINAL

NO MIDDLE NODE   MIDDLE NODE   MIDDLE RAREFACTION   MIDDLE CONDENSATION

© 1990 by TOPS Learning Systems

LONGITUDINAL WAVES Sound (   )

1. Set a can with both ends removed on clay supports. Hang index-card circles from narrow hinges of masking tape over each end. Make a smaller flap and a larger lid as shown.

2. Surround the can with your paper spring. Tape the end of each straw to the table.

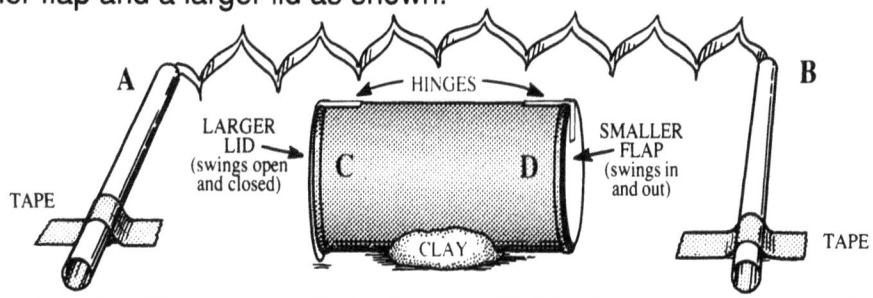

3. Tap sharply with your pencil at A to move B. Must a paper coil move the entire distance from A to B in order to transfer the energy across? Explain.

4. Tap lightly with your pencil at C to move D. Explain how squeezed-together air (a condensation) transfers energy through the can similar to a paper spring.

5. Quickly open the lid at C. Explain how stretched-apart air (a rarefaction) transfers energy to the flap at D.

6. Using dots to represent air molecules, draw how several sound waves might look as they move through the can.

© 1990 by TOPS Learning Systems

PITCH PROBLEM (1) Sound (   )

1. Push the end of some heavy string and light thread (about 1/2 m long) through a hole in the end of a can. Tie both strands to a paper clip.

2. Hold the can near your ear as you strum each strand. Experiment with different ways you can make high and low pitches.

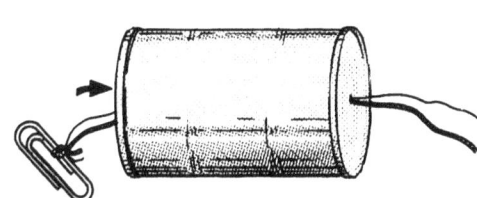 

3. Name 3 different variables that raise and lower the pitch of vibrating strings. Complete the table.

4. As the pitch of a vibrating string is raised or lowered, what happens to its frequency?

VARIABLE	To raise the pitch…	To lower the pitch…
a.		
b.		
c.		

© 1990 by TOPS Learning Systems

PITCH PROBLEM (2)   Sound ( )

1. Blow across the mouth of an empty soda bottle to make a whistling sound. Then add a little water and blow again. As you repeat this process, what do you notice?

2. Slowly add water to a glass while tapping its side with a spoon or fork. What do you notice?

3. Why does pitch increase in one case and decrease in the other?

© 1990 by TOPS Learning Systems

RESONANCE   Sound ( )

1. Tightly hold 3 clothespins to the bottom of a can with rubber bands. Label them A, B and C.

2. Unbend 3 bobby pins. Clamp 2 into A and B at the last "ripple" on the wavy end. Clamp the third into C at the next-to-the-last "ripple."

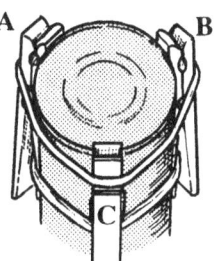
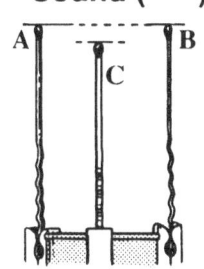

3. Measure all 3 pins to be sure A = B > C. Which pin sounds at the highest pitch? Which sound at the same pitch? Explain.

4. Strum each pin, 1 at a time, as you hold the can in your hand.

a. Which pins resonate (vibrate together) even though you strum only one? Which don't?
b. What do resonating pins have in common? Explain why this is so.

5. Adjust 2 soda bottles with water (if necessary) so they have the same pitch. While a friend blows a note on one bottle, hold the mouth of the second bottle first close to your ear, then away. What do you notice? Why?

© 1990 by TOPS Learning Systems

cards 13-14

BEATS ○ Sound ( )

1. Cut out all 5 frequency strips. If each line represents a wave crest, and each number counts a second, write the frequency (in Hertz) at the top of each strip.
2. Rub oil on each strip so the paper becomes semi-transparent.
3. Press these strips together (2 at a time) so the seconds line up. Hold up the paper to good light to observe how the wave trains *beat* (bunch and spread).

   a. Fill in the table: count the beats/second between each pair of strips.
   b. What mathematical regularity can you discover?

	8 Hz	9 Hz	10 Hz	12 Hz
8 Hz	b/s	b/s	b/s	b/s
9 Hz		b/s	b/s	b/s
10 Hz			b/s	b/s

4. Layer together 6 pieces of masking tape about finger length: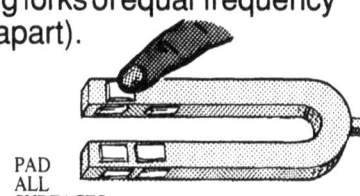

5. Get 2 tuning forks of equal frequency (or 1 octave apart). Cut narrow pads of tape to attach to *one* of the forks. PAD ALL SURFACES

6. Strike both forks. Hold them near an ear like this and listen to the beats.

7. How does the frequency of these beats change as you remove pads of tape? Use your results from step 3 to explain your observations.

OCTAVE RULES ○ Sound ( )

1. Flag 3 pieces of wire with masking tape that accurately measures each length.

2. Tightly hold 3 clothespins to the bottom of a can with several rubber bands. Clamp a wire into each clothespin so its measured length is free to vibrate.

3. Strum each wire while holding the can to your ear. What is the relationship between its length and its pitch?

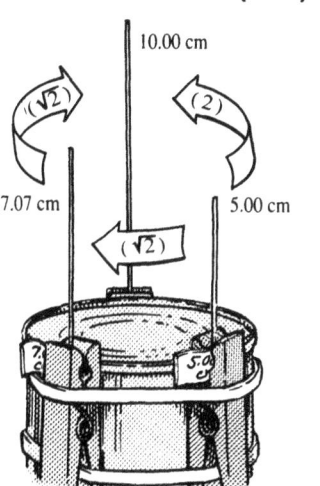

4. Adjust 3 more untagged wires so they sound 1 octave apart. Confirm that the ratio of their lengths is close to the predicted values.

5. Each new higher octave vibrates at twice the frequency of the previous lower octave. If middle C vibrates at 256 Hz., what is the frequency of...
   a. high C.   b. low C.
   c. one octave below low C.

cards 15-16

HOW LOW CAN YOU GO?   Sound ( )

1. Adjust a wire to sound at middle C (256 Hz). Accurately measure the length of the part that is free to vibrate.

2. Repeat 2 more times. Choose your most consistent result or find an average.

Trial	Length (cm)
1	
2	
3	

3. Apply this result plus your octave rules to complete this table.

frequency (Hz)	256	128	64	32	16	8	4	2	1
length (cm)									

4. At what frequency does the wire vibrate too slowly to hear? (What is your lower threshold of hearing?)

5. Measure out enough wire to vibrate at 1 Hz. Confirm that it really does.

ON THE RECORD   Sound ( )

1. Build this phonograph.

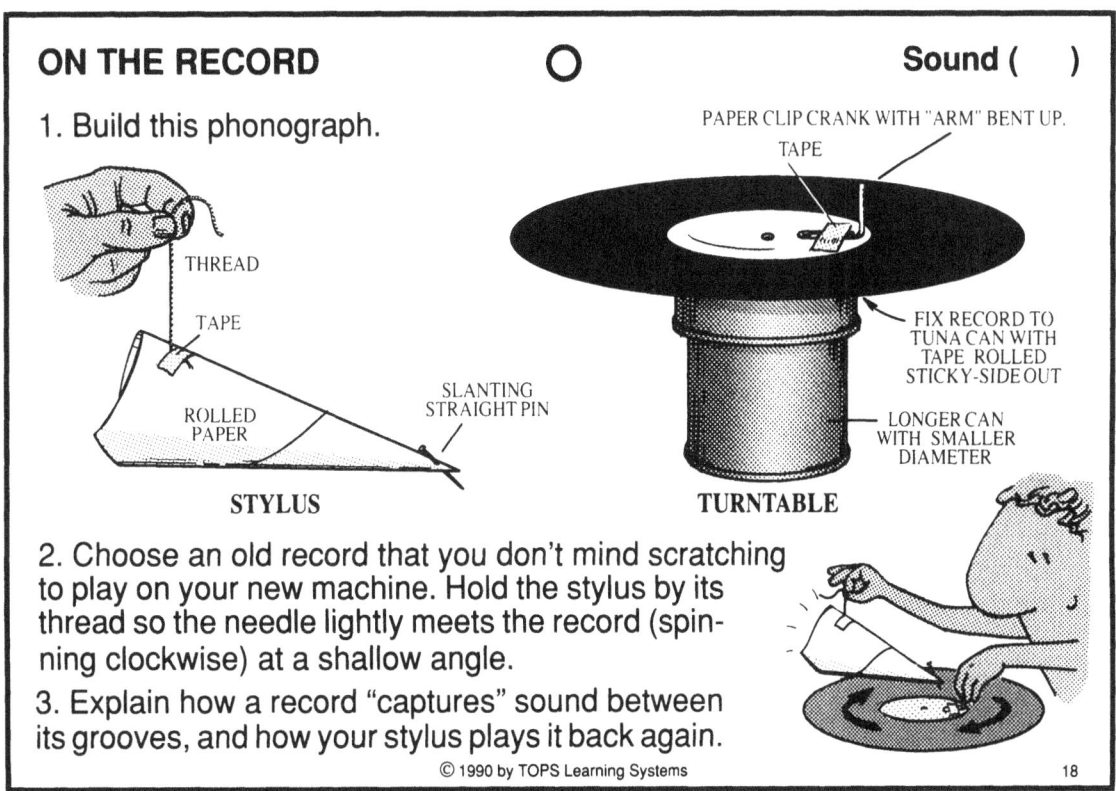

2. Choose an old record that you don't mind scratching to play on your new machine. Hold the stylus by its thread so the needle lightly meets the record (spinning clockwise) at a shallow angle.

3. Explain how a record "captures" sound between its grooves, and how your stylus plays it back again.

REED MUSIC   ◯   Sound ( )

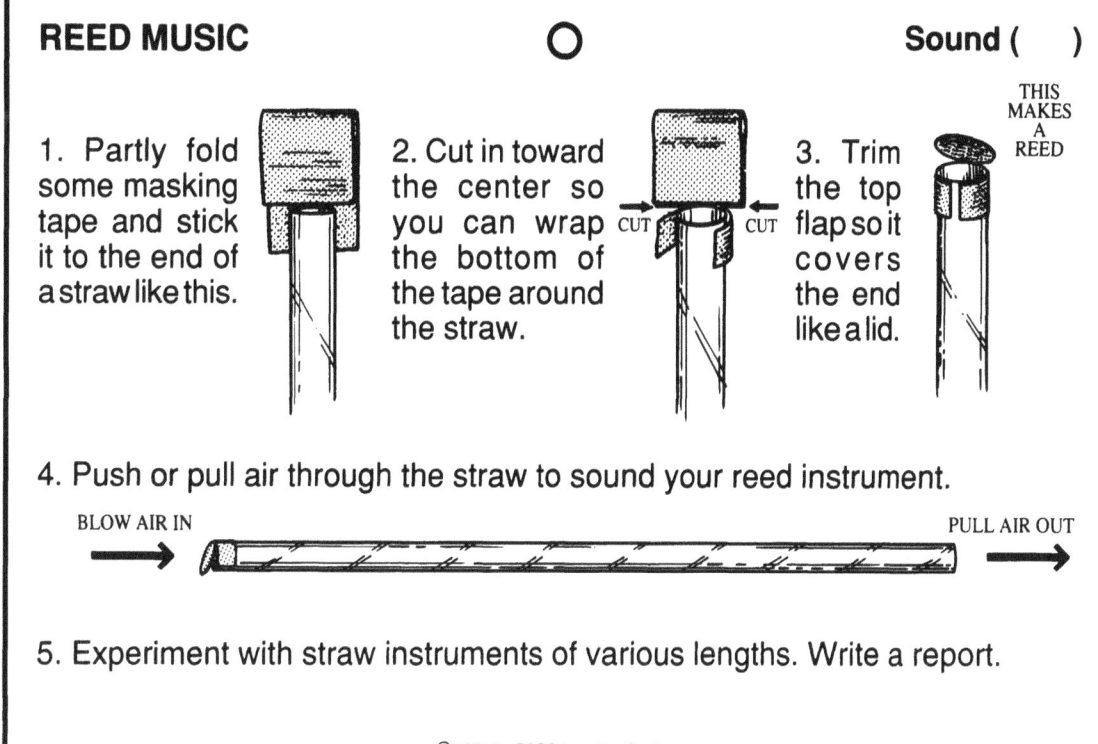

1. Partly fold some masking tape and stick it to the end of a straw like this.
2. Cut in toward the center so you can wrap the bottom of the tape around the straw.
3. Trim the top flap so it covers the end like a lid. THIS MAKES A REED

4. Push or pull air through the straw to sound your reed instrument.

   BLOW AIR IN →   PULL AIR OUT →

5. Experiment with straw instruments of various lengths. Write a report.

© 1990 by TOPS Learning Systems

SPEED OF SOUND   ◯   Sound ( )

1. Stand far enough from a wall or building so you can hear a distinct echo when clapping wood blocks together.

2. Clap these blocks just fast enough so the returning echo is totally drowned out by the sound of the next clap. Measure this frequency in claps/minute.

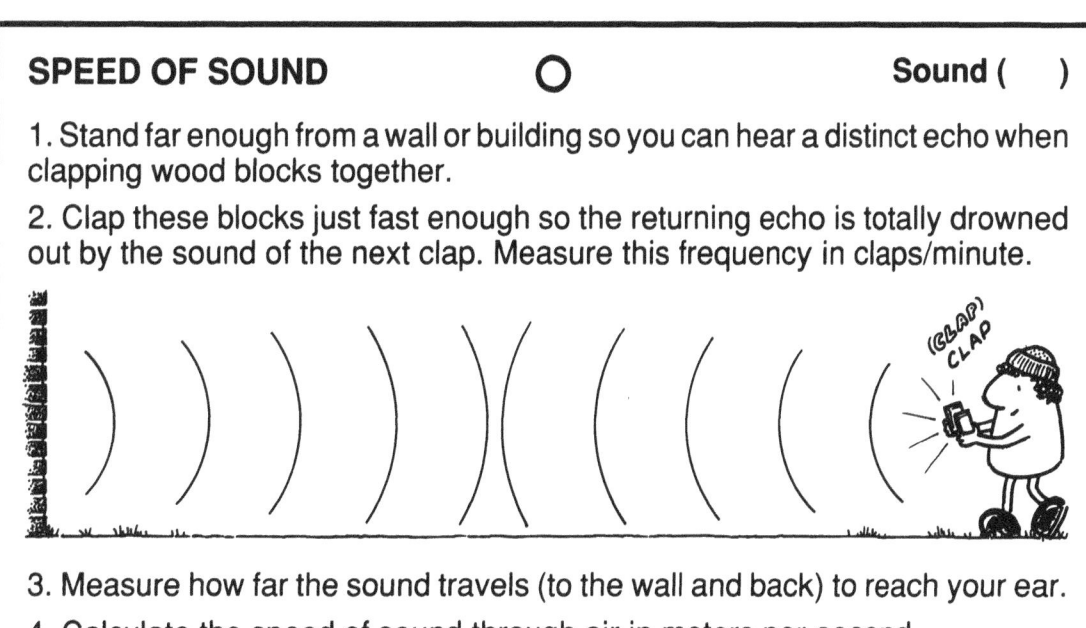

3. Measure how far the sound travels (to the wall and back) to reach your ear.

4. Calculate the speed of sound through air in meters per second.

$$\frac{meters}{sec} = \frac{meters}{clap} \times \frac{claps}{min} \times \frac{min}{sec}$$

© 1990 by TOPS Learning Systems

Supplementary Cutouts

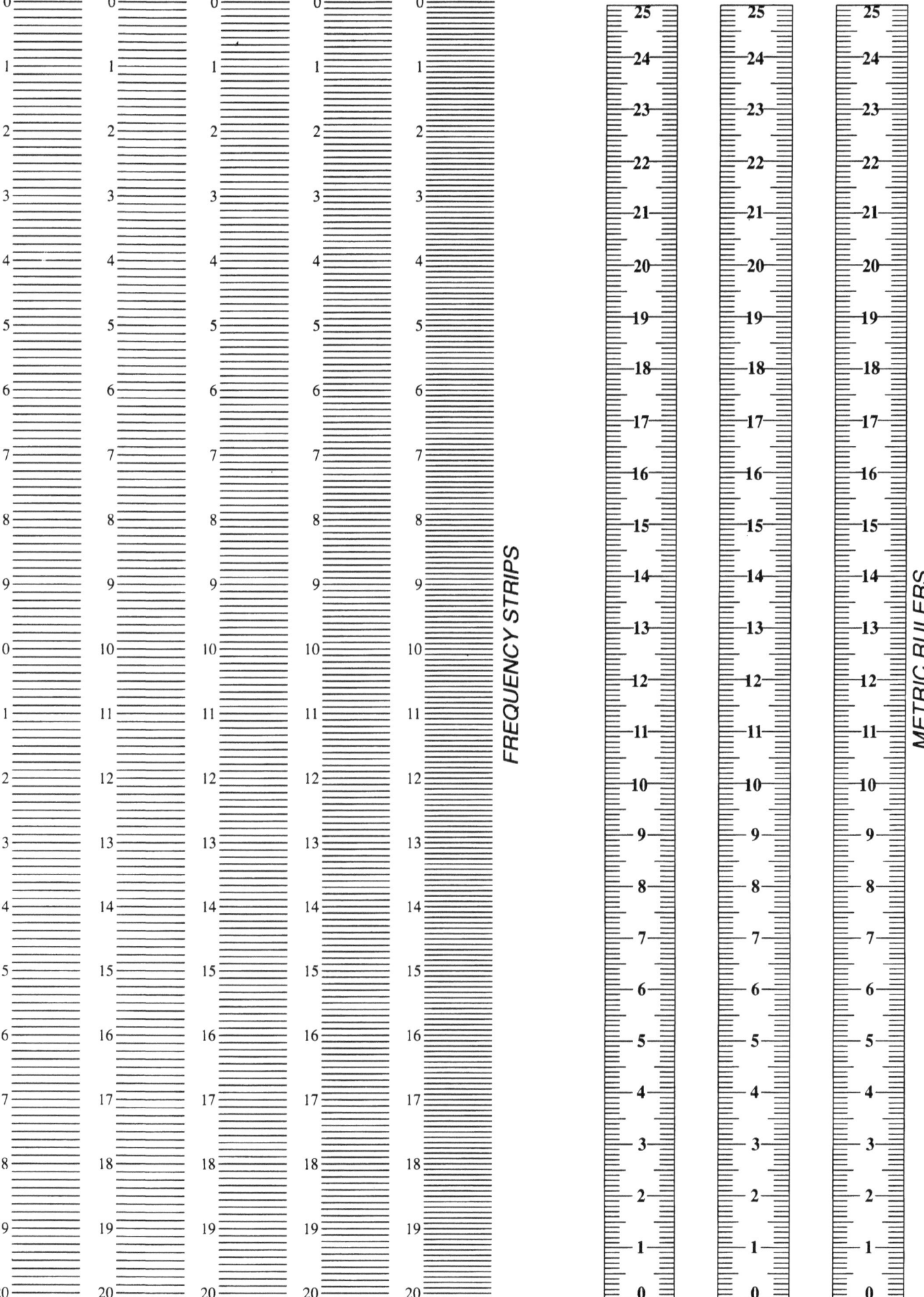

Feedback

If you enjoyed teaching TOPS please tell us so. Your praise motivates us to work hard. If you found an error or can suggest ways to improve this module, we need to hear about that too. Your criticism will help us improve our next new edition. Would you like information about our other publications? Ask us to send you our latest catalog free of charge.

For whatever reason, we'd love to hear from you. We include this self-mailer for your convenience.

Sincerely,

Ron & Peg

Ron and Peg Marson
author and illustrator

Your Message Here:

Module Title _____ Date _____

Name _____ School _____

Address _____

City _____ State _____ Zip _____

———————————————————— FIRST FOLD ————————————————————

———————————————————— SECOND FOLD ————————————————————

RETURN ADDRESS

_____

_____

_____

PLACE
STAMP
HERE

TOPS Learning Systems
342 S Plumas St
Willows, CA 95988

TAPE HERE

www.ingramcontent.com/pod-product-compliance
Lightning Source LLC
Chambersburg PA
CBHW080554170426
43195CB00016B/2790